A WAKE-UP CALL FOR T

I WAS MUCH
HAPPIER
WHEN EVERYTHING
I OWNED WAS
IN THE BACK
SEAT OF
MY VOLKSWAGEN.

RICHARD ROBERTS

BABY BOOMER PRESS

Requests for permission should be addressed to: Baby Boomer Press, P.O. Box 290145 Charlestown, MA 02129. Call: 1-800-507-1968

Baby Boomer Press books are available in quantity discounts for sales promotions, premiums, fund-raising and special events. Please contact the publisher for details.

Visit: BabyBoomerPress.com

Printed in the United States of America
First Paperback Edition
10 9 8 7 6 5 4 3 2 1
Designed by Neville Design
Production by NetPub.com
Photography by Christian Delbert

First Printing April 2004

ISBN: 0-9749659-0-1
Library of Congress Control Number: 2004091022

DEDICATION

This book is dedicated to
the self-reliant spirit of
the Baby Boomer generation.

CONTENTS

I WAS MUCH HAPPIER WHEN EVERYTHING I OWNED WAS IN THE BACK SEAT OF MY VOLKSWAGEN.

WAKE-UP CALL FOR THE BIGGEST GENERATION

> We are stardust,
> We are golden,
> And we've got to get ourselves
> Back to the garden.
>
> —Joni Mitchell, "Woodstock"

Well, we're not the "greatest generation." Tom Brokaw says so and he just may be right. Understand I've got nothing against my parents and their cohorts. They won the Big War and I never mention the fact that up until Pearl Harbor the vast majority of them wanted nothing to do with the conflict. Nor do I point out that after Pearl Harbor two-thirds of our soldiers were still draftees, not volunteers. Today's seniors also lived through the character-building Great Depression. My father and mother were, respectively, fifteen and ten years old in 1935, not exactly the middle of the economic mainstream, but again, not something I dwell on.

As a WWII veteran, my father received a free, four-year college degree, $90/month spending money and a guaranteed VA housing loan at two and one half percent. As a Vietnam era vet, I got $315 a month for nine months to finish grad school. When I tried to buy my first home, VA loans were capped at $70 grand, which didn't get you a covered parking space in downtown Boston at the time, and no lender in the city was interested in doing business via the government. My father got a parade and a life. I got three grand and the right to re-grow my hair.

Still, no sour grapes. My folks were lucky enough to come of age in a world that wasn't shadowed by atomic weapons, international terrorism, backbreaking taxes, technological disorientation, flesh-eating viruses and a spy-on-you government. Tom's a good journalist; he might have mentioned that. Nevertheless, I gave my parents his book as a present and I'm sure it made them feel proud.

Listen up, Tom: Those are bellbottoms, peasant blouses and white bucks back on store shelves. The VW Bug and Microbus are rolling off assembly lines. The Thunderbird designed as a roadster, not an aircraft carrier, is back. Don McClean's *American Pie* is backing up the latest TV ad for Chevy Cavalier and that's Led Zeppelin's music in a Cadillac spot. Last Thanksgiving they ran an Elvis special in prime time, a programming decision usually reserved for his birthday in January. Simon & Garfunkel are back on tour! Those are Rock-at-50 and Folk-Rock specials raising money on PBS.

We Boomers are the targets again, and it's not National Guardsmen shooting at us this time. When we develop a need, or cop a notion, or decide to act, there's just no ignoring us. We made civilization safe for Rock and Roll, hula-hoops, Frisbies and flu shots. We redefine every stage of aging in this culture. We did the revolution thing, the accumulation thing and now we're about to redefine retirement, the third stage of our fabled lives. Not enough to be the greatest generation? O.K., but keep in mind there are billions of dollars and social upheaval hanging on our every move.

You've heard the joke about how if you can remember the Sixties you weren't really there, but one memory lingers inside me like a Joni Mitchell lyric. It's a feeling of happiness. A persistent, growing, unrestrained joy. That was ours once fellow Boomers. A sense of possibility and the feeling that there was more, much more, to come. We knew we were exactly in the right place at the right time, and there were enough of us to make a difference.

Even better, with possibility came purpose. History had called upon us to re-assert fundamental civil rights; the right to be told the truth in a Democracy, to question the hypocrisy of our leaders and institutions, to expose the untrustworthy prevailing order. Is there anything sweeter than the pursuit of truth and justice? Could there be anything about this country more valuable or more worth preserving than personal freedom?

We raised holy hell. We challenged everything. Sex, education, family relations, journalism, women's rights, social priorities, and most of all, how Americans would forever after view their relationship with government. We didn't give a damn about history, or how it was supposed to be. The more established it was, the more suspect it became. We were willing to change things and live with the consequences.

When Nixon appeared on TV, we jeered and threw roaches at the screen. When our draft boards beckoned we burnt our selective service cards, cut off our toes and trigger fingers, drugged ourselves up to fail their profiling tests, or piled into our Volkswagens and headed for Toronto. When our parents threatened to cut off the tuition, we conjured up the terrifying specter of us lounging around the rec room back home.

What longhaired, disrespectful, arrogant rabble we were — and the best-educated, most optimistic, most liberated generation in history. Some would say we were just over-privileged and had nothing to lose. We had plenty to lose — our lives, for instance. And we had the music to eulogize our plight. Don't bother to point out that the country wasn't greatly advanced by the words to *Itsy Bitsy Teenie Weenie Yellow Polka-dot Bikini.* Think Dylan, Elvis, Simon & Garfunkel, Janis Joplin, Grace Slick, Hendrix, The Beatles, The Who and The Stones.

C'mon, Tom, the Lennon Sisters?

True, we're not exactly leaping out of bed these days propelled by unrestrained joy, or dedicated to preserving American ideals. Some of us can hardly get out of bed. We're bogged down with possessions and disrespectful kids, daily calendars, bulging midriffs and an endless, almost hopeless, array of entanglements and investments inside the society we once vehemently condemned.

It's easy to argue that idealism is for the young and with time and age we abandoned our dreams just like every generation before us. We got co-opted. Before he died, Curt Cobain accused his Boomer parents of something much worse: perverting the American dream, not just abandoning it.

The news isn't all accolades to be sure. Our endless questioning of authority seems to have turned into a perverse lack of respect for everything and everybody, not just politicians and lawyers but teachers and social workers as well. Our love of rebellion has 24% of today's eighth graders smoking dope and drug use among teens up 100% in the past ten years. Our vaunted liberalism has lowered social standards to the point where it's easier to get out of a marriage than a Tupperware contract. And our former distrust of materialism has evolved into some grotesque fetish to label rather than live our lives.

It would be nice to blame the godless Communists, but ever since Billy Boy was in the White House, it's been our watch. We are the government that's now controlled by 20,000 paid lobbyists. We are the people, a third of whom now draw a paycheck directly from Uncle Sam. Our current president, whom a lot of us Boomers voted for, is running around in cowboy boots and a flight jacket he didn't earn; some very upset foreigners are bombing our buildings and the general population, that's you and me, is walking around in its sleep. Alarmed academics have declared this a national malaise—*cultural somnambulism*. It means we can no longer tell fact from fiction, and we're starting not to care. We're shutting down.

It's been a quick ride down a bumpy slope. Sort of like the second act in one of those Roman epics with a cast of hapless millions looking the other way as outside events come rushing in and everybody thinks someone else will surely know what to do. Wouldn't count on the U.S. Congress—the current gang has a code of conduct that would make the Irish Travelers blush. Or Wall Street, which seems determined to exterminate the entire middle class. And our religious leaders? Well, they've apparently been screwing us, too.

I'm even starting to see the patriotism that came out of Sept. 11 as twisted and profane and that worries me as a veteran. "Buy some jewelry or a new car, or the terrorists win..."— pretty damn sure I don't like the idea of having my role in this society reduced from concerned citizen to consuming unit. Is this any different than the Chinese government telling their people, which they did, to eat rats to help stop a growing infestation? The Chinese government at least published recipes. We got a national mood ring—the Department of Homeland Security's five-color terrorism bar code, *so they can tell us how we're supposed to feel.* Remember when we didn't take this kind of advice from authority figures?

Not exactly the world we were planning on leaving our kids, huh?

There's still time, but not much. Time to reclaim the heady confidence of our youth. Time to rekindle the remarkable spirit that once earned us leading roles as the authors of what's happening, what's relevant and what's cool. It's time to shed our generational apathy and disassemble the institutions that, by and large, have failed us miserably over the past three decades.

We know where we're going after all, we've been there before. We were right in the Sixties and history proved us right. Johnson and Nixon *were* lying. Vietnam *was* a crime. Blacks and women *needed* liberation. People and planets need love. Henry Kissinger *didn't* deserve the Nobel Peace Prize.

If we don't change the agenda, who will? We change everything we touch. We've transformed jobs in big business with creative thinking, flextime, casual dress Fridays and chaos theory. We've reconciled investments in corporate America by demanding ethical conduct be an essential component of corporate identity. We've disrobed organized religions and found comfort in our own spiritual paths. We've reconciled $40,000 kitchen and $20,000 bathroom makeovers with the need to stay in touch with our bodies and ourselves. We've legitimized "alternative" everything and forced entrenched institutions to adapt to our needs. We've kept a love of the natural world, eastern philosophy and global thinking alive. We put the eco in tourism and the sport in utility vehicles.

Who tells us we can't have it both ways? Our generational history is one triumph after another. We've built successful careers not only by railing against the establishment, but also by competing against millions of our cohorts. We're sharp and battle tested. Sure our kids are a mess, but, hell, so were we.

Back in the Sixties we had energy and imagination and nerve. Today we have power and money and perspective. If it takes votes, we represent them. If it takes bucks, we've got'em. If it takes time, we've got more and more of that, too, and we sure as hell have nothing more important to do with it. As David Brooks said in his fine book, *BoBos* in Paradise,* if Boomers "raise their sights and ask the biggest questions, they have the ability to go down in history as the class that led America into another golden age."

Even if you weren't in the streets during the Sixties, don't tell me you can't remember the feeling of being part of something important. The rush of blood, the moral clarity. The smell of smoke, the sounds of sirens. We were forged into a single mind by the significance and intensity of those days. That gift is still inside us, churning in our guts, etched in our psyches, written in the margins of our old journals and on our keepsake album covers. It's what makes us sleepless today. The turbulence and life-and-death issues we faced were real. We faced them together. Don't forget there are still 76 million of us, and that makes us The Biggest Generation.

I remember as clearly as yesterday the freedom of having everything I owned in the back seat of my Volkswagen. It was religion-like. When Gandhi died all he owned was a spoon, rice bowl and an extra pair of sandals. He had never held political office. Never advocated violence or raised an army. He drove the British army out of India by practicing a simple philosophy: You must be the change you wish to see in this world.

That kind of personal conviction starts with awareness and that's why I wrote this book. To challenge each and every Boomer to ask tough questions. Where am I really at? How many of the things I own really matter? How numb have I become to anything outside my immediate world? What moral example am I setting for my kids?

We don't have to hit the streets again (but remember, it makes good TV). We can affect change with our votes, our checkbooks and through our jobs, influence and the media. We can do it because *our* generation is the social conscience of this society. You don't have to agree with everything I say in this book and we don't have to all think alike. We share the same generational ideals, nevertheless—they're alive inside us like an inner voice. A voice that's telling you and me and every other Boomer that America is better than this. That it's always better when we're involved. We need to wake up, care and get involved again.

As the saying goes, If not Boomers, who? If not now, when? We made a good start back in the Sixties, but the job is only half done.

Imagine the satisfaction in completing it.

CHAPTER 1

ARE YOU SAFER NOW THAN YOU WERE TWO YEARS AGO?

You tried to make
A good thing last,
How could something so good,
Go bad, so fast?

—Neil Young, "American Dream"

I am writing this in the fall of 2003, and the nation has recently marked the two-year anniversary of Sept. 11. The media has been filled with retrospectives and reports on our progress against international terrorism. You don't need a national poll to tell "safety" is the number one issue on the public mind.

How 'bout it? Feeling safer?

Not if you saw two recent *ABC World News Tonight* segments: One reported on undercover agents who presented phony documents at Motor Vehicle Departments across the country and got back legitimate U.S. drivers licenses 100% of the time. The other showed how *ABC* employees arranged to smuggle a spent-radiation device through the screening machines at a major U.S. port. The embarrassed government's response? Investigate *ABC News* for terrorist activity.

The fact that the Patriot Acts have non-governmental "officials" intercepting and overhearing private conversations and correspondence—maybe yours—shouldn't make you feel safer either. Neither should the Gallup poll that showed 63% of Americans feel the invasion of personal privacy these Acts allow is justified.

White House spin—have you noticed that "searching for weapons of mass destruction" has become "searching for *evidence of programs to develop* weapons of mass destruction?"—not only doesn't make me feel safer, it pisses me off.

Then there's the story about how a student named Nathaniel Heatwole repeatedly breached airport security over an eight-month period carrying aboard box cutters, a knife, bleach, matches and a reddish clay that looked like C-4 explosives. He even wrote federal authorities notifying them of his actions, and got no response. Not the kind of courtesy we can expect from real terrorists. Then there was the guy in New York who packaged himself up in a crate and flew undetected through four airports. How about the fishermen who wandered around the runways at JFK airport for over an hour without anyone noticing?

Feeling safer, or just stupid for standing in two-hour lines at checkpoints knowing full well that, as *TIME* magazine in their November 3, 2003 issue reported, "thousands of low-paid workers have carte blanche to roam airports, ramps and runways without undergoing personal inspections or having their belongings checked." All this at airports where we've been concentrating our efforts. Live near a port, or nuclear power plant? Got kids in school in New York City?

While we assembled nearly 200,000 people in the new Department of Homeland Security, the GAO recently set up a phony corporation to see if it could buy biotech materials over the Internet to make bombs. Turns out, you can. And guess who from? From our own Department of Defense! It's running a web-based store for evaporators, centrifuges, all kinds of bio gear, and they're letting it go at bargain basement prices. Just perfect for the price-sensitive terrorist market.

The big picture stinks, too. Back in the 1960s, according to Oxford Professor Niall Ferguson writing in *The New York Times*, the richest fifth of the world's population had a total income 30 times as great as the poorest fifth. By 1998 that ratio was 75:1. Not exactly a stabilizing trend, and one that's getting worse here at home.

Even the advertising community, which as a rule is persuasive about anything, has stumbled. Charlotte Beers, one of Madison Avenue's brightest stars, accepted a position as Under Secretary of State for Public Diplomacy and Public Affairs. Her task? To create and broadcast commercials explaining the wonderfulness of America to Arab-speaking peoples. She has now resigned. Her commercials have been withdrawn, too, after everyone agreed they completely missed the point.

Hollywood, bless its socially conscious heart, is trying to help. For the new Fall Season we have, among others, Kiefer Sutherland in *24*, a show about our "last line of defense against terrorism." And there's *Threat Matrix*, hour-long stories about folks who "will stop at nothing to keep America safe." Fiction is more comforting than the truth these days.

There are new products out to make us feel safer: portable nerve gas and anthrax detection sensors, personal ballistic shields, gamma radiation alarms, anti-microbial hand creams, skyscraper escape devices and homing beacons you can strap onto your kids. Plus there's been a revival in home survival and catastrophe kits, portable generators, bomb shelters (isn't that nostalgic?) and a big run on latex gloves.

Somehow…

The list of things to worry about is as open-ended as the task of trying to safeguard an open society. Even Defense Secretary Rumsfeld is having second thoughts. His recently leaked memo questions whether his policies, indeed our whole post-Sept. 11 effort, have been (as he might himself put it) off target.

One thing surely is. Where is the outrage in response to being duped, cajoled, lied to and intimidated by our leaders?

Where does the Oregon state legislature, for example, get the nerve to propose a bill that warns protestors who interrupt civil affairs with activities like traffic jams shall be labeled "terrorists" and sentenced to a minimum of 25 years in jail? Isn't that exactly the kind of governmental tyranny we're fighting over there? We've wasted the last two years asking ourselves how to stop terrorists rather than asking why they want to blow us up in the first place. As anyone with an undergraduate degree in psychology can tell you, if you're attacked—even if you regard the attack as completely unwarranted—the most important thing you can do is ask yourself what *you did* to become the target in the first place.

On the *AMC Channel*, reporter Charles Stuart asked just that when he wondered, "What effect does the flood of American media have on the ultra-conservative Muslim world?" What indeed does a culture where women are covered by veils, where not just pre-marital sex but even dating is routinely considered immoral, think of the silicone busted babes of *Baywatch* with their nipples poking through bright red Lycra® swimsuits. While you're at it, ask what are the effects of U.S. military bases dotting the Mideast landscape, the roar of F-15s overhead, our aircraft carriers and destroyers cruising offshore, and our bombing Iraq at will for over a decade?

Answer: shock, resentment and hatred. And we'd feel the same damn way if the situation were reversed.

You may remember what happened to Bill Maher, host of HBO's *Politically Incorrect,* two years ago. When one of his guests called the Sept. 11 terrorists cowards, Bill observed that perhaps it took more courage to fly a plane into a building than it did to press a button and watch a Cruise Missile disappear over the horizon. This comment caused outrage. *HBO* received complaints from Republicans, Democrats, political action committees, the Department of Defense and a stream of god-fearing, flag-waving Americans. Bill was forced to publicly apologize; *HBO* cancelled his show anyway.

Some time later, as a guest on the *Chris Rock Show*, Bill asked his host, "Shouldn't there be at least one place on the dial, one show amid the official lineup, that questions the mainstream line of fluff and orchestrated bullshit?"

Apparently not.

Radical Islam is not the real danger to America. Our unwillingness to examine our proper place on this planet is what's scary. To ask whether or not exporting mostly guns and sex-drenched videotapes is worthy of the most power-ful nation on earth. To ask ourselves why anyone would find the World Trade Towers, symbols of our prosperity, so offensive they were willing to go to almost unbelievable lengths and self-sacrifice to destroy them.

You needn't expect any help from our invested institutions. Detroit will continue to seduce us with gas guzzling SUVs. Hollywood will continue to soothe us with unreal reassurance. Religion will comfort our sorrow and bury our dead, but distort the argument. And the federal government will continue to reassure us in documents that invite no debate like, "The Progress Report on the War on Terrorism" that was just released. It reads like the bright shining lies of Vietnam.

We Boomers must be willing to ask ourselves the tough questions. We must try to see ourselves as others see us and understand how we have failed in their eyes. To understand whom we are, not just as Americans but also as earthlings. Ask what it means to be human.

In the past two years I have seen hundreds of hours of up-close and personal stories documenting the tragedy of Sept. 11. I have read dozens of articles that analyzed economic consequences down to the penny and political fallout down to a single vote. There's been more empathy than you'd find at a UFO conference in Roswell. Compassion, patriotism, generosity, bravery are there. But in all of it I can't find twenty minutes of hard-working self-appraisal.

Other than Chris Rock, nobody has expressed much public sympathy for Bill Maher either.

If you, like me, think asking little old ladies to take off their shoes in airports accomplishes nothing other than giving the terrorists a good laugh, read on. Safety isn't the main problem facing this country, and we Boomers must, because we're the only ones who can, change the dialog in this country.

Remember when we used to get together with cardboard and markers to draw up signs? We created an entire lexicon of slogans and symbols that are still recognized the world over. We communicated an entire philosophy with "Make Love Not War." We rallied against official establishment drivel with tighter thinking and more compelling ideas. We were raised on television and we understood how to use its impact to our advantage.

We're experts in making what's on our mind the national agenda.

CHAPTER 2

THE NATURAL ORDER OF
THINGS TODAY

"It's one, two, three...what are we fighting for?"

–Country Joe McDonald, "I-Feel-Like-I'm-Fixin'-To-Die Rag"

Remember the scene in the movie *Network* when the Peter Finch character, Howard Beale, infuriates the executives who run his TV station? He questions the impending deal between the imaginary UBS Network and its giant holding company, CCA. Finch has been given leeway to tell the truth on his TV show because his ratings have skyrocketed. But when he calls for a public protest to stop Western World Funding Corporation from buying CCA because they secretly represent Arab interests, management decides it's time to reprogram their Howard Beale puppet. Finch is led upstairs to a dimly lit tapestry paneled conference room where CCA Chairman, Mr. Jensen, played by Ned Beatty, awaits. Beatty delivers one of those magnificent world-view rants only Paddy Chayefsky, the movie's screenwriter, seems capable of penning:

You have meddled with the primal forces of nature, Beatty warns Beale, and I won't have it. You are an old man who thinks in terms of nations and peoples. There are no nations; there are no peoples. There are no Arabs, no Third World, no West. There is only one holistic system of systems, one vast interwoven, interacting, multi-varied, multinational dominion of dollars...petrodollars, franks, deutschmarks...It is the international system of currency which determines the totality of life on this planet. That is the natural order of things today.

Bush, Cheney, Halliburton, and Bechtel. With France, Germany, Russia and China, investors in Iraqi oil production, objecting to our intervention. A single dominion of petrodollars.

When Ross Perot ran for President in 1988, he made a bold suggestion to raise the price of gasoline to $10 a gallon. He contended this would help solve many of our most pressing domestic problems: air pollution, traffic congestion, debilitating insurance rates, endless lawsuits, repair bills, oil spills, commuting nightmares, epidemic stress, teenage accidents, four-car families, and so on. Side effects would include lowering costs of oil-based products like plastics and fertilizers and medical equipment, not to mention how a reduced reliance on automobiles would put millions in disposable income back into the hands of ordinary folks. Here, Perot also argued, was an opportunity to make foreign policy based on something other than profligate ways. A way to loosen the noose the Middle East holds around our collective necks. The simplicity of the idea was dazzling. The logic, unassailable. Perot was written off as a nut.

I have a lake house in Maine where I go for peace and quiet. I go to hear the hoot owl that sits in a nearby tree and serenades the neighborhood. I go to hear the sound of wind whistling through the tall pines, the chirping birds and the gentle drip of rain and lap of waves.

What I also hear are the sounds of lawnmowers, leave blowers, chain saws, hedge cutters, off-road vehicles, motorcycles, weed wackers, bush wackers, roto tillers, back hoes, chippers, skidders, tractors and haulers, boat engines and the incessant rev of jet-skis screaming across the water from dawn to dusk. Has there ever been a more annoying, unnecessary, polluting, loon and fish killing invention than the jet-ski?

In winter, out come the snowmobiles.

Here we are, fifteen years post Perot, fully one-third of our national economy dedicated to the internal combustion engine, and our boys and girls fighting a how-do-we-get-the-hell-out-of-here war to keep gasoline at $1.69 a gallon. Given the cars we drive and how much we drive them, it all seems justified. We hand over tens of millions of dollars every day to Arabs dazzled by the good fortune of having found a people willing to pay $30 a barrel for the stinky, undrinkable goop that lies beneath their desert sand.

Oil companies buy up promising energy alternatives like public transportation and photovoltaics to make sure they never flourish. They raise the price of gasoline in *anticipation* of a coming shortage. They buy politicians who solve our energy problems by opening up more wilderness lands to exploration while the White House legally maneuvers to keep the minutes of the Vice President's Energy Task Force meetings a secret.

Oil corporations will tell you flat out they don't consider themselves to be American companies. There are no nations.

We Americans need our jolts. We need to think fast, move fast and be first in the competition. And we need energy to do it. How else can we remain the most powerful nation on earth? Detroit hears our plea. In the past twenty years, the average horsepower of an American automobile has doubled. And Detroit is promising us cars with 500 and even 1000 horsepower in the near future.

The next time you get behind the wheel of your car, ask yourself: What is the natural order of things? Ask yourself about oil and Iraq.

The public debate about this war can drive you crazy—I mean that literally. Are we there to finish the father's business? To rescue a tortured population from a sick dictator? Because Iraq defied U.N. resolutions? To keep America safe? To protect our friends in the Middle East? Is our presence an essential part of the international war on terrorism?

Or is it because America runs on oil? Like it or not, that's the way it is. Blame whomever you like but first take a look in your garage. Take oil out of the American economy and the system shuts down within months, maybe weeks.

Everything stops. Basic services like heat, water and electricity. Trucking, ports, commuting, tourism. The financial markets. Your job. It's societal Armageddon time.

Now imagine the closed-door conversations of the Energy Task Force that the White House is desperate to keep secret. Imagine the men who run Big Oil advising the President and Vice President. It might have gone something like this:

> Gentlemen, Venezuela, a principal source of oil imports to the U.S., cut off all production because of internal political upheaval earlier this year. With the collapse of the Soviet Union, Russian oil fields are mismanaged and deteriorating. There are huge reserves but frankly the Chinese, Indians and Russians will get there before us. In Kuwait, our friends are under increasing pressure from religious fundamentalists to whom they are making one concession after another. Iran, as you know, is part of the 'axis of evil' and does us no good. Indonesia, with substantial reserves, is a Muslim nation teeming with Al-Queda operatives. Saudi Arabia, our primary source, apparently has been financing terrorists from the beginning and the royal regime is so far removed from its radical Muslim population that Osama bin Laden himself predicted it will fall within our lifetime. Mexican production is unreliable due to political corruption. Pirates are highjacking more and more ships, including oil barges, in the straits of Malacca through which half of the world's oil travels.

Environmentalists have vowed a long fight to keep additional American reserves in wilderness areas from being developed. Lastly, our country's emergency supplies would, frankly, be used up before most of us lower our thermostat.

We're not in Iraq to finish daddy's business, a largely romantic notion. We're not there to remove a dictator — perhaps you've seen the videotape of Rumsfeld shaking hands with Saddam back when we were selling him arms to fight the Iranians and gas his own people. We didn't care then and we don't care now. In fact, we rather like dictators. The U.N.? Recent events will tell you how much we care about its opinion. To fight the war on terrorism? Hell, before we took over Iraq there were more Al-Queda in Buffalo than there were in Baghdad. To protect our friends in the Middle East? Who was Saddam going to invade? Russia? Syria? Saudi Arabia? Iran? He tried that, remember?

We're in Iraq for the oil. The U.S. Army is now sitting atop the world's second largest reserve of high quality crude. Tens of billions of barrels and Bechtel and Halliburton, our commercial defense department, are over there right now patching things up. The war in Iraq is a pre-emptive strike, not to stop the development of weapons of mass destruction, but to guarantee America a steady supply of oil. We're not there to steal it, we're there to put it back on the market. And the cost? Given the size of the reserves versus the cost of the war, about a dollar a barrel. An absolute bargain.

This is what was said in those private meetings. Bet'cha a tank of gas.

Trying to make sense of any other explanation, no matter how well orchestrated or how often repeated by this administration, is crazy-making. It's the kind of newspeak George Orwell warned us about, and Chayefsky wrote about. It contributes directly to our current state of confusion and disorientation. It helps explain the level of shrill in our public discourse. As former Colorado Governor Richard Lamm put it, "America's energy policy is zigzagging through history like a drunk."

Most of Europe and every Muslim on the planet believe we're in Iraq for the oil. They're absolutely right.

If our nation's leaders aren't going to lead us, then we have to lead them. It's time for each of us to adopt an individual energy policy. Take serious steps about weaning ourselves off gasoline and oil. We can stop taking unnecessary trips and combine our errands. We can carpool. We can walk more and ride a bike, or take public transportation. We can get rid of gas powered contraptions. We can shovel and rake rather than blow and shred. We can add passive solar to our homes and invest in alternate energy companies. We can, acting together, start to break the stranglehold Big Oil has on this country.

We can act, or sit around until the day the lights go off and all we have in the cupboard is one can of tuna and an electric can opener.

CHAPTER 3

WHY THE C-SPAN CAMERA NEVER MOVES

Clean up your own backyard
Oh don't hand me none of your lines
Clean up your own backyard
You tend to your business. I'll tend to mine.

—Elvis, "Clean up Your Own Backyard"

Every week *TIME* magazine asks someone important ten questions. On November 3, 2003, they asked Walter Cronkite "What is the most underplayed story today?"

"Congress," he said.

You better believe it. That may be one reason why the following Internet memo has been so widely circulated in recent months. I can't attest to its accuracy, but given the performance of the 535 current members of the U.S. Senate and House of Representatives, I have little reason to doubt what it said about them:

• Twenty-nine have been accused of spousal abuse.

• Seven have been arrested for fraud.

• Nineteen have been accused of writing bad checks.

- One hundred and seventeen have been involved directly or indirectly with a bankrupt business.

- Three have done jail time for assault.

- Seventy-one have such bad credit they can't get new credit cards.

- Fourteen have been arrested on drug-related charges.

- Eight have been arrested for shoplifting.

- Eighty-four have been arrested for drunk driving.

- Twenty-one are currently defendants in lawsuits.

Don't forget, these are folks who are writing and passing the laws that you and I are required to follow!

Congress spent its first 70 years building America by passing the Bill of Rights and opening up the West. Almost ever since, its been exploiting the wealth of this country. The grand hall, once occupied by orators like Webster and Clay and Adams, has been largely reduced to empty suits standing before a C-SPAN camera yakking at empty seats. Legislation as an art of debate or compromise has been replaced by a pre-occupation with character assassination extending from Watergate right through the Clinton administration. Anything of consequence is being said in the back room.

Today, when our so-called representatives should have their collective mouths wide open over the incredulity of administration policies, only a few veterans in the twilight of their careers like Robert Byrd have had the mustard. The rest cower in embarrassment or concern for their careers. Often, they're absent.

It's time for Boomers to vote for someone, anyone, else. Greens, Libertarians, Reformers, you name it. It's time to get over our automatic coronation of incumbents in the two major political parties in this country. The Republican and Democratic National Parties are *not*—this may come as a surprise to you—officially part of our government. They are, in fact, businesses, private corporations. They're rich, powerful and have usurped real representative government by pushing through election rules that discriminate against independent candidates. This, despite the fact that 37% of Americans call themselves Independents, not Republicans or Democrats.

Our founding fathers never intended for America to be represented by career politicians. Neither this Congress, nor any future one, will ever pass term limits on themselves. But a voting block of 76 million Boomers can un-elect them all. We know all about grass roots politics. In the Sixties we worked from the bottom up and the outside in and look how effective we were. Now our jobs and connections put us in a position to influence things from the top down and from the inside out.

Know how to whistle?

CHAPTER 4

MUSICAL CHAIRMEN

And no one's getting fat 'cept Mama Cass.

—The Mamas & The Papas, "Creeque Alley"

B ill Moyers is one of the few believable journalists still working on TV. You may have heard him report on a growing cancer in our representative system of government recently—that is, it's no longer representative. Rather, it has evolved into a private club comprised mostly of corporate influencers who buy the allegiance of government officials, actually help write the laws, and marginalize political opposition.

The relationship between money and politics, always a threat in our country, has become an addiction. Politicians now spend up to 50% of their time raising the millions needed for re-election. Most of this money comes from special interest groups and this, in turn, allows many individual and industrial contributors to operate with total immunity. One fact alone illustrates how disease-ridden our political process has become: In 1968 there were only a handful of registered lobbyists in Washington; today there are over 20,000.

Just who are they?

Lawyers, of course, and public relations executives, heads of trade associations and former corporate executives. But many more are former government officials—from White House staffers, ex-cabinet members, congressional aides and committee staffers to (and this is the best of all possible resumés) ex-Congressmen and women. According to reporter and educator Martin Gross, "...about half of all departing Congressmen become lobbyists and they're the best in the business." Why? Because as privileged alumni they can, for the rest of their lives, freely enter the House or Senate chambers *even when Congress is in session.* Perhaps with their arm around someone they'd like to influence. Perhaps whispering something in their ear just before a vote is taken.

When you're in, you're in.

These inside players glide effortlessly between positions in government, law firm partnerships, consulting gigs, lobbying groups, non-profit causes and special interests all without changing golf partners. It's like having your own private military-industrial-Congressional complex. It's like playing musical chairs where they *add* chairs.

The New York Times' profile of President Bush's Energy Department is a perfect example of how the game is played:

- Assistant Secretary Rebecca Watson is the former president of the Reason Foundation, financed by oil and mining interests.

- Senior Advisor to the Secretary is Alaska's ex-senator, Drue Pearce.

- Camden Toohey, Special Assistant to the Secretary, used to be the executive director of Artic Power, a group that endeavors to expand drilling in Alaska.

- The Deputy Secretary is a former member of a lobbyist firm that represented the National Mining Association.

- The Secretary herself, Gale North, received some $286,000 from the energy industry during her Colorado U.S. Senate campaign.

(Any more questions about the Bush administration's real intentions toward our environment?)

This merry-go-round of influence peddling exists in every cabinet, department and agency of our government, at virtually every level. Many players have worked for both the Democrats and the Republicans so the music never stops. In his new book, *A National Party No More*, Zell Miller, the Democratic Senator from Georgia, reveals how corrupted by money and pressure the system is on both sides of the aisle. "The process is so politicized that that can't be put aside even in times of war," he told Jon Stewart on *The Daily Show*.

Bill Moyers thinks it's become so insidious, so indifferent to representing the public interest that he came right out and asked on his PBS Show *NOW*, whether, "there's even anything resembling democracy left in America?"

Surely not in our Department of Defense. Insiders refer to the Pentagon as "Versailles on the Potomac" because of the mirrors (get it?). The Pentagon's annual budget of $400 billion plus has more than a little to do with the legions of ex-generals now working for defense contractors. Hey, as an ex-sergeant in the U.S. Army I'm for a strong national defense. But better foot soldiers are the least of what we get for all that money.

Listen: According to a former Pentagon employee and long-time critic of the system, Franklin Spinney, there's essentially no control over projects. Budgets are, using his word, "fiction." The Pentagon can't even audit its own books. They simply have no record of where over $1 trillion has gone. Amazingly, they admit it. So here's what they did: they relaxed their own auditing standards! And did so with the blessing of the Senate Armed Services Committee and various House subcommittees that are supposed to be keeping an eye on things for you and me. That's right; in the face of 10-figure mismanagement they changed the rules to become even less accountable to the country.

The reality is this: it's in the insiders' best interest to keep the money flowing. Congressional members get projects for their districts. Lobbyists earn their keep. Defense contractors keep unnecessary or outdated projects alive. Lawyers get huge fees for haggling over contracts.

The vaunted Missile Defense System serves as an example. It's failed so many field tests, the military put homing devices on the targets so they'd be easier to hit. And future tests have been declared a matter of national security so no outsider can witness them or report on the results. This is the kind of well-entrenched policy that covered up the fact that the M-16 rifle constantly jammed in combat, one more reason some friends of mine died in Vietnam. And as I'm writing this, Assistant Secretary of Defense Paul Wolfowitz is on Capitol Hill presenting a bill to further reduce oversight on Pentagon spending. You see, he has Iraq to finance.

Today there's more secrecy, less disclosure, less transparency and more ways to hide money than ever before. In the Defense Department and everywhere else in government. And more and more money. The politically driven economy in Washington isn't affected by natural market forces, or kept honest by public scrutiny. Around town they call it a "self-licking ice cream cone."

Hard to be more cynical than that.

Imagine: over one billion dollars a day on national defense and another billion every day in deficit spending. For $300 toilet seats, new fighter planes, nuclear submarines, an intercontinental ballistic missile defense system, and God only knows what else. Doesn't scare Osama bin Laden.

The American war machine didn't scare the North Vietnamese 40 years ago either. It's time for Boomers to remind politicians who haven't learned from history something we understood in our youth. It is ideals that make a nation great and hold it together, and they are bulletproof.

CHAPTER 5

WAS JACK RIGHT?
CAN WE HANDLE THE TRUTH?

We can try to understand The New York Times' effect on man.
Whether you're a brother, or whether you're a mother,
You're stayin' alive, stayin' alive.

—The BeeGees, "Stayin' Alive"

We stretch the truth in America: *This little beauty has only eleven thousand original miles on it...The magic potion in this bottle solves exactly your problem...The Promised Land really is right over that hill.* We don't mind a little hucksterism. Around these parts, it's suckers and buyers beware. As Ziggy, the cartoon creation of Tom Wilson, put it, "Honesty is the best image."

A few years back I got a lesson in honesty on the way home from work. I had stopped at a grocery store in the nearby Charlestown section of Boston to pick up something for dinner. The store was nearly empty and unusually quiet. In the produce aisle I discovered why. A tall Black man suddenly broke the silence by yelling at a little old lady who was scurrying away as fast as she could push her cart.

Don't you look at me. I see you looking.

You don't see many Blacks in Charlestown. It's a traditionally Irish neighborhood—tough, secular, and by and large unwelcoming to the ongoing gentrification by Yuppies. For a Black man, or any outsider, to call attention to himself by intimidating local shoppers is a noteworthy collapse of common sense.

As I worked my way through the produce aisles, our eyes eventually met and sure enough I received the same don't-look warning.

Know what I think? I called back.

What? He was clearly surprised I'd answered.

I think you're mad at somebody else.

Hey man, he said with a big grin, *you tell the truth.*

The truth. It seemed a strange answer until I started thinking about all the noise, slick language and seductive imagery that surrounds us. We are awash in misinformation, much of it intentionally bad. Experts on the same subject agree on almost nothing. Large organizations—governments, corporations, churches and powerful individuals alike—have always had plenty to hide and plenty of convincing ways to spin facts to their advantage.

But we're losing our grip on the truth in more insidious ways. Dignity is a matter of photo IDs and 16-digit identities. We're wired and more connected, but the communication is more impersonal. Authentic replicas have become more popular and more accessible than originals. We brand ourselves rather than seek individuality. Fleeting pixels have replaced hard copy. Programmed telephone systems and artificial intelligence provide more answers. Virtual reality is so real; *The New York Times* reported that artificiality, itself, "becomes the star."

What are even less obvious are the systemic changes in our society that have created new ways to manage and mold the truth. Consolidation, conglomeration, inter-networked communications have conspired to create a new kind of mass awareness in America. One that allows no unsponsored messages. Or debate. Not exactly Big Brother, but Big Brothers. A kind of Orwellian oligarchy with the same stultifying effect. "We're being relentlessly told the exact opposite of what's really happening," Jon Stewart, host of *The Daily Show*, put it. Here's how it works:

Chance has been eliminated: Interviewed on PBS during the summer of 2003, Mike Deaver, former Ronald Reagan handler said, "The last thing we ever wanted in the White House was an unplanned moment, a genuine impulse, a dramatic, honest event." He went on, "the truth was never allowed to compromise the mission." This isn't just policy on Pennsylvania Avenue. Everything a modern CEO, CFO, spokesperson, politician, institutional or cause leader says (think of your twelve year old kid quoting a catchy ad slogan) is well rehearsed and well polished. Responses, particularly in government, come from a constantly updated list of official answers that are often designed to evade unwanted questions. Bush cabinet member Condoleezza Rice, for example, is known around town as the Fourteen Phrase Lady. And those not polished in minimizing embarrassment or avoiding meaningful discourse never get in front of a microphone in the first place. The effect? No unplanned communications. No accidental peek at the truth.

And that beautiful turkey George carried into the mess hall on his surprise visit to Baghdad over Thanksgiving? A theater prop. Not edible. The only thing being stuffed here is your mind.

With less and less institutional independence, time-honored sources of objective information are disappearing: Universities and agencies once dedicated to pure research now take so much public and corporate money that research conclusions are often foregone. Surely honest academic investigators remain, but many have fallen prey to commercial rewards. Unfortunately, you can take almost any desired result and work backwards to design an experiment that proves it. More often than you think, so-called scientific research is based on the opinions of just a handful of participants.

Independent research firms have been gobbled up, too. The advertising business, for example, is no longer just in the business of making advertisements. Take Torre Lazur-McCann, a worldwide advertising agency specializing in healthcare, for example. It's been buying up medical journals, drug development companies, scientific labs and clinical studies companies. It owns Target Research, a company that tests new drugs, perhaps some that Torre Lazur is advertising. Or, take the giant ad conglomerate Omnicom. It owns Scirex, a research company that tested the drug Bextra®, which happens to be an Omnicom client. Or take WPP, another advertising giant whose empire includes IntraMed. What the public doesn't understand is that these ad agencies indirectly employ or contract retired doctors to write reviews about medical products. Doctors are the kind of folks Americans like to trust. I'm not saying that there's any direct pressure put on a particular doctor to express a particular opinion, what I'm saying is that many doctors working for these once-independent research companies have quit since their purchase by ad agencies.

This matrix of influence exists in every industry today. Corporations, agencies and groups the public still sees as disparate, and therefore objective and trustworthy, are, in fact, increasingly tied together in partnerships and alliances and agreements and often part of the same corporate family. Do you think you'll ever hear any serious criticism of major tourist attractions or the cruise industry on *ABC World News Tonight* now that Disney owns the network? Or a nasty inside look at General Electric by *NBC Nightly News?* When I started out in advertising, editorial departments never talked to the ad side of the business. Editors were protected as journalists. Now commercialism of media is overt and unapologetic. Half of what's presented as editorial today is really advertising in disguise because it's part of some deal.

Content is evolving toward one big "program note." Only a handful of financially independent publications and broadcasters still exist, and most, unfortunately, are backed by one-sided causes with no intention of being objective. Carl Bernstein, famous for Watergate, was recently quoted in the *New York Sunday Times* in an article entitled, "So much for 'The Front Page.'" He observed, "The standard for journalism used to be 'What's the best obtainable version of the truth?'…Now we're living in a celebrity culture that no longer values truth more than hype."

No wonder so-called experts can't even agree on a diet that works.

The media and the government are increasingly on the same side: The Federal Communications Commission recently pushed hard to allow further consolidation of mass media in this country. It was a move that was enthusiastically supported by media lobbyists like the National Association of Broadcasters (NAB). Tape, aired on major news networks, showed FCC Chairman Michael Powell (Secretary of State Colin Powell's son, by the way) claiming that further consolidation would actually *increase* competition. A little hard to believe given that cable rates are already rising four times faster than inflation. A little hard to believe given that 40 of the top 50 cable channels are owned by the six giants that control all the major TV stations and cable companies. The mass media provided the airtime for the FCC chairman but virtually no criticism of his absurd argument. The FCC, after all, has taken some 1400 "trips" at the NAB's expense.

If you want a disturbing look at how concentrated owner-ship of local media keeps the truth hidden, pick up a copy of Jim Bouton's new book, *Foul Ball*, which relates how a compromised town council, monopolistic control over the *Berkshire Eagle* newspaper, the General Electric Company and a large New York publisher all worked together to keep the people in Pittsfield, Massachusetts from knowing that the local ball park they were being asked to purchase was a toxic waste dump.

Another example: In Hillary Clinton's latest book, *Living History*, she tells about her surprise and shock upon discov-ering Bill's philandering. She repeated this in an interview with Barbara Walters, who was in turn interviewed on the same point by Tom Brokaw of *NBC Nightly News*. I'm not pretending to know what Hillary may have known, but I wonder why everyone else in the country, or at least in Arkansas, was better informed about Bill's sexual proclivi-ties than she was. Anything from wishful thinking to revisionist history passes as truth these days, especially when it comes out of the mouths of authoritative personali-ties, and then gets repeated again on the evening news.

We are exposed to hundreds of spokespersons that are afforded credibility just because they're on television. Influencers are provided airtime because of who they are, not on the merits of what they have to say. As Mike Deavor explains, "the press corps covers government events accompanied by 'government minders.'" It's *your* mind they're talking about. This increasing compliance of network news departments may help explain the immense popularity of Jon Stewart's news parody show on *Comedy Central* that regularly does a better job of exposing the truth about world affairs than mainstream media. And people know it.

Big business and government are increasingly on the same side: If you think you've finally figured out what "lite" and "healthy" and "natural" on food products mean, think again. Expect to see scores of new health claims in ads and on packages under a new FDA policy that allows food processors to make claims that are backed by less than "significant scientific agreement." This puts food in the same regulatory space as supplements, where promises run from the sublime to the outrageous. I get at least one email a day promising to improve the size of my manhood, a claim I soon expect to see on a box of Frosted Flakes.

Trusted brands can't be trusted. Little lies add up. Just ask the telecom industry which has discovered that pennies per person can mean millions in profits. Tom Brokaw reported on the *NBC Nightly News* in a "Fleecing of America" segment that AT&T and Lucent have deceived 10 million customers of some $47 billion—at least this is the contention of a class action suit alleging that AT&T never informed customers of their option to buy, rather than continue to rent at outrageous fees, old telephones. Little old ladies had paid thousands for a $29 Princess Phone.

60 Minutes took the telecom business to task, too, years before the WorldCom collapse, declaring that the industry was "over-extended, in debt, top heavy and criminally controlled." CBS included the market's largest and best-known brands in its allegations. Vendors were billing people who weren't their customers, forging signatures on agreements, switching people between services without notifying them, engaging in blatantly deceptive advertising, even charging customers for the company's unrelated real estate costs. Like I say, these weren't boiler room operations. These are the companies you're likely buying your phone service from. These are the folks who gave us the lies called *FCC Line Charge, Universal Service Fee, Local Number Portability, 911 Enhanced Surcharge, Federal USF Surcharge, Universal Service Fund,* and *School and Library Fund*—all of which cost you money every month. And on cell phone bills there are actually charges for product development. That's right, you're paying for features that aren't even available yet, and you'll pay more when they are. Here's what's true about your phone bill: it's gone up.

Wall Street is in on the action, of course. A little game they call "late trading," which is illegal. They place orders to buy shares as late as 6:30 PM, but at 4 PM closing prices. This enables them to make money on any intervening news since most corporate news is released after the market closes each day. Practices like this, according to New York Attorney General Eliot Spitzer, bilk investors out of billions annually. If you've got big bucks to spend, the boys in finance have got a bigger and better deal for you called Tax

Shelters. For millions in fees, they'll move money around between cooperative third parties like major banks and law firms so you can avoid paying taxes on, say, the sale of a large asset. Ernst & Young, as reported recently on *60 Minutes,* is particularly good at this. The IRS has taken an increasingly dim view of these practices, contending that while a given activity might not violate a particular statute of the tax law, it certainly violates the spirit of those laws. The practice is so widespread, however, many millionaires take the chance. Should you fail an audit, the IRS will not come after Ernst & Young, but they'll come after you. Turns out, no one prosecutes the designers and marketers of these schemes because the laws aren't written that way. Of course not, the major auditing houses and financial firms wrote the laws or influenced the legislators who did.

What makes for good drama contributes to our confusion: The widely circulated story of Private Jessica Lynch's ordeal in Iraq is a case in point. Early reports of her being shot and stabbed and slapped around apparently weren't true. We were fed verbal images of this tough, female soldier, machine gun firing from one hip, mowing down advancing enemy troops until she ran out of ammo and injuries brought her down. Then there was the follow-up story about our special forces fighting their way into the hospital to rescue her. Also a lie. True, the mass media recanted their early reporting, but only briefly except for *60 Minutes.*

We like the fictional version better. That's the story we wanted to hear, not how she got hurt when her Jeep rolled over, or how she missed the entire battle, or that there was no one guarding the hospital. Problem is, it's not the job of journalism to provide dramatic non-fiction. That's the job of the publishing industry, and thanks to ongoing adoration on network television and a TV-movie deal, Knoff has offered Pvt. Lynch a $1 million advance to tell her story in a book. Pvt. Lynch has an admittedly fuzzy memory of that time, but that won't keep Knoff from making a buck. Suffice it to say phrases like "true-life TV movie" are reality-bending concoctions, and you can be sure the TV production of *Saving Jessica Lynch* wasn't held up by a lot of fact checking.

Speed contributes to misinformation: The Internet has given us Urban Legends and fake web sites. Years ago, *The Blair Witch Project* was heavily promoted on the web as a true story before its release as a movie. That set a standard. There are now innumerable web authors with no credentials. Photography can be manipulated at will. There are phony sites that purport to sell the eggs of famous and beautiful models for artificial insemination. Another describes how the National Security Agency is secretly reverse-engineering extraterrestrial spacecraft. It all contributes to the noise.

Systemic changes can create pop-up industries based on intriguing but questionable theories. You can have a book, company, lecture series, press conference, web site, a hundred media bookings and be already working on a follow-up book before your theory is ever put to real world tests. The business community is awash with examples. The so-called creativity-in business-movement is one. Millions in books and seminars were sold on the proposition that everyone is creative. The premise? Businesses have overlooked a fertile source of productivity and profit — namely, the creative thinking of their rank and file employees. Maybe. If you mean by "creative" everyone has ideas, sure. But are they creative ideas? Or just unusual? Or maybe not creative, but certainly examples of creative thinking. And who's to decide? Some consultant? Want a creative idea for your business? Put up a suggestion box.

The parapsychology business is another pop-up industry rife with bad science and outright baloney that gets widely publicized. Recently a friend of mine attended a conference for so-called intuitives. The highlight of the two-day seminar was a test of the collective intuition of the audience. The seminar leader wrote down five psychological disorders and placed them in sealed envelopes. She then asked for total concentration and then went around the room asking people what was written down. She took several answers for each envelope, and sure enough, the audience successfully intuited what was in all five envelopes.

This of course is a parlor game. The instructor has done this exercise dozens of times before and she already knows what her audience is likely to guess. Plus she can throw in a hot topic; maybe drop a hint or two in previous lectures, or during hallway conversations. Maybe provide a handout. The attendees were, according to my friend, delighted.

They had thought so. They really *were* intuitive. That's what they had paid hundreds of dollars to hear.

And if you want to tell a lie and be believed, tell a big one. Try watching cold reader John Edwards on his popular TV show, *Crossing Over.* He talks to the dead. Strangely, they have nothing interesting to say.

Marginalization of alternative thinking can also make the real truth seem unlikely: When Black activist Louis Farrakhan appeared in Boston in October 2002 he asked, "Why invade Iraq? To what end? Clearly this country is no danger to us." A wide-eyed local TV reporter followed Farrakhan's remarks with the comment, "Radical? You bet." Much opinion that runs contrary to the mainstream is presented as the work of dangerous minds by our media. Farrakhan also remarked that he felt President Bush was a greater threat to world peace than Saddam Hussein. A lot more people agree with him today than when he first said it in Boston two years ago.

Meanwhile any pinhead with a loud mouth can find a public forum. Criminals, con-artists, paid flacks with transparent motives, people with well-documented psychological problems, and run-of-the-mill whack jobs hyping themselves or a dubious cause get plenty of space and air time. Often the logic presented is about as intoxicating as a BYU pep rally. Instead of being better informed so we can cope, our mind space is taken up with errors, trivia and prejudice. Plenty of surveys illustrate this. I like the one that says ten times more people know who the "sock puppet" is than can identify the Prime Minister of Canada. A cynic might conclude that the media's saturating coverage of stories like Michael Jackson's sex life, Paris Hilton's risqué videotape and more about Monica Lewinsky than anyone needed to know is one way to keep the public from knowing anything of consequence.

To gauge how accepted dishonesty has become as an operating premise in this society, you need look no further than the enormously popular TV show, Joe Millionaire. Joe's life is a charade, the contestants are duped, the audience plays along with the deception and they call it "reality programming."

Spin makes us dizzy: As I recall, it was journalist H.L. Mencken who observed that the principal task of government is to keep the population in a constant state of alarm. So far, it's been a banner decade for the feds.

As our current U.S. Attorney General put it on August 3, 2003, "There is a very real possibility that Al-Queda could strike the United States." This inane comment aired on every major news network that night. No commentator observed that there is a very real *possibility* almost anything *could* happen. No editor decided this pandering to public fear didn't deserve airtime in the first place. After all, it was John Ashcroft speaking. In a recent interview, documentary filmmaker and author Michael Moore suggested why,

"As a society we endorse being sold fear...So many different groups benefit from the public being afraid."

I'm not a big believer in conspiracy theories, but let's face it: They're confiscating our money, restricting our freedoms, increasing surveillance over our movements, and pumping us full of lies and medications. Isn't that what they do in insane asylums? Gore Vidal calls what's happening in this country a slide into "despotism." It isn't too strong a word.

That evening in Charlestown, the police eventually showed up and dragged the Black man out of the grocery store right past me. He smiled again and called out, *Hey Bro.* It occurred to me that he'd been driven wacky by all the lies. Like a Chinese water torture, the drip, drip, drip had finally gotten to him. He never heard the truth. As a Black in America, almost everything he heard was a lie. No authority was reliable. No potion was going to solve his problem. The Promised Land was a myth—and only a myth. The same thing is happening to us all of us. As James Bovard warns in his latest book, *Terrorism & Tyranny,* the government is becoming more powerful and the people more ignorant. The worst thing that can happen in a democracy.

How much of our disorientation and fear is caused by trying to absorb stories and explanations, facts and statistics that we know don't make sense? The expert packaging and orchestrated delivery of misinformation in this country is creating popular somnambulism. We're swimming in genetic fallacies, generic fallacies, and the eight other abuses of logic my old ethics professor warned me about. We're at war with the very institutions designed to protect us and we're going nuts. In self-defense, we're shutting down.

Just when did we Boomers start buying the official line? Have we forgotten the stream of lies that poured out of Johnson's and Nixon's and Kissinger's mouths? A recent Gallup poll says 69% of us think the Patriot Acts may not go far enough!

Listen: It's no longer a matter of some snake oil not living up to the promise on the label. Now it's our retirement plans. Now it's our trust in each other, our institutions and our personal freedoms. Now it's our souls and our sanity.

The next time the Democrats say that over three million jobs have been lost in this country in the past two years, ask them why the Republicans claim the real number is only 75 thousand. And ask yourself, how the hell they could be so far apart? And next year, when President Bush stands up in a Midwest manufacturing plant on Labor Day and declares, "Economic indicators are rising faster than expected," don't believe it just because it's want you want to hear. Or because it's on the news. Or because he's the president. Ask yourself what indicators? Faster than who expected? Ask yourself how much conviction he has in what he's saying. And the next time you turn on your TV and hear a phalanx of government officials all repeating the same phrase over and over, understand this is a pubic relations assault, not just a policy initiative. The more people talking like parrots, the better the chance whatever they're saying is a lie. Weapons of mass destruction? Sure. Probably on the way over from New Jersey right now.

This country is losing its diversity of thought, and with that you get duller thinking, lowered values and less criticism. Redundant, unexamined reporting by our mass media amounts to a single state-run outlet. We receive "unfiltered feed." With the politicalization of the message, opinions become headlines. Conclusions become inevitable and personal options get eliminated. We lose our sanctuaries as individuals. We become afraid.

We proved once that real power in this country resides with the people. We have ceded too much of it to Washington. We can take it back by telling the truth. First to ourselves and then to anyone who'll listen. Just think back to the days when you stayed up all night with your friends arguing about the future of America, penning new slogans and planning your next demonstration of free speech. The days when you helped make the collective voice of our generation an unstoppable force.

CHAPTER 6

HOW THE STREET BEAT YOU

It's time for a walk on the real side
Let's admit the bastards beat us
I call to dissolve the corporation
In a pool of margaritas.

—Steely Dan, "Everything Must Go"

How's your 401k? Pissed? Hard to believe, but apparently Wall Street spent the past 20 years convincing middle-class Americans to invest in stocks just so they could—systematically and acting together—steal them from us. Every major bank and financial house on The Street has been accused of illegal conduct. Even the mutual funds. The dot.com bust is bigger than all the financial scams from Tulips futures to Black Friday combined. Not the kind of activity that's going to restore my faith in institutions. Our ever-vigilant government (which covets your retirement accounts as much as Wall Street, by the way) has worked out a $1.5 billion settlement with The Street on your behalf. In case you missed some of the details:

First, only about $450 million of the $1.5 billion will go to settle lawsuits filed by investors. According to *The Wall Street Journal*, the rest, over a billion, is earmarked for something called "restitution, education and dissemination of 'independent' research.'" And this sum, with the blessing of Uncle Sam, will be tax deductible for The Street so their actual total costs will be closer to $1.1 billion. Plus, Wall

Street will receive insurance payments to lower the penalty even further—in the end, considerably less than $1 billion. When you consider the collective rip-off of the American public was in $2 trillion range, you have to admire the way these guys can manage money. Kind of makes you wonder who was arguing on our behalf. Suzie Orman?

Of course, there's been a lot of bad publicity regarding certain corporate executives and their financial goings-on. Some of these folks may be forced to hold up on their Aspen estates after the season ends. There's that. And we can take comfort in the fact that we've captured their ringleader: by the time you read this, there's an excellent chance that Martha Stewart will be doing time. Probably whipping up some osso buca in her cell toilet or wrapping the bars in festive crepe paper. Nobody is above the law, our government reminds us. Martha would have been a lot better off if she had stayed a broker.

My father warned me when I was young that stockbrokers don't know anything. If they really did, they'd be breaking the law. But, probably like you, I was seduced by their slick come-ons, the mahogany paneled offices and the parking lots outside filled with Mercedes coupes. I was pretty sure if they were "Bullish on America" they were going to be bullish on me. As the joke goes, the only thing I got dealing with a broker was broker. It didn't start out that way. Early in my career I had a terrific broker at Merrill Lynch who took me to lunch, listened to my aspirations and helped me build a small nest egg. He took the long view, put me mostly in Blue Chips and from time to time would call with advice to buy a particular stock that usually made money. When he retired I was turned over to a hot-shot rolodex jockey whom I never met and was willing to sell me anything, usually some security Merrill was "making a market" in. By the time he got done managing my future, my savings had lost a decimal point. I got rid of him in favor of someone who was soon fired over philosophical differences—not hard to imagine. In the Wall Street slim down after the dot.com boom my account was then handed off to a client services pool somewhere in New Jersey. The last time I talked to one of these kids it was to request a report I needed for tax returns. It never arrived. Bull is bull.

In retrospect, the best stock tips I ever received were from friends and casual acquaintances. The co-worker whose father had just started a company that went on to introduce three well-known brand names. The woman to whom I gave directions one day walking down the street and she rewarded me with news about a small company that had just received off-shore oil drilling rights in the Gulf of Mexico. The stock tripled by the end of that week. And the tip from a friend who knew her public company was about to start buying back its own stock.

In April 2002, *The Wall Street Journal* retired its famous Dartboard. This feature pitted expert stock pickers against a random selection made by tossing darts. Over 142 contests, the *Journal* reported, the pros did outperform the darts—posting a 10.2% gain versus 3.5% for the darts. But there were plenty of weeks when pure chance outperformed the experts—55 out of 142, in fact. And when weekly gains were measured in the 0-24% range (which was most of the time) the pros only beat dumb luck by a single percentage point.

You want a good stock tip? According to U.S. DataStream, the market performs much better on sunny days in New York City than on cloudy days. From 1982 to 1997, cloudy days averaged just an 8.7% increase versus 24.8% for sunny days.

Did your broker ever mention that?

Remember the scene in the movie *Wall Street* when the good broker, played by Hal Holbrook, says to high-flying but dishonest Brad Fox played by Charlie Sheen, "A man stands on the edge of the abyss. He looks down and sees nothing. In that moment he discovers his true character." Charlie says he thinks he understands.

Do you? Have you looked into that empty 401k and found your character?

A $1billion slap on the wrist isn't going to reform Wall Street. It says, in fact, they get to keep 99% of everything they stole. Sure, brokerage firms have increased oversight and downsized their analyst departments, but they're not getting out of the business. And the new Accounting Oversight Board, put in place by the SEC to police the accounting industry, picked

William Webster to head it up, a man under suspicion for accounting irregularities at his own former company. They chose not to appoint John Briggs, a man regarded as independent enough to be a real reformer. Former SEC Chairman Harvey Pitt made the final decision. He did so not long after taking a meeting with U.S. Representative Michael Oxley (R-Ohio), chairman of the House Financial Services Committee and the number one recipient of campaign donations from the accounting industry.

Not too comforting that the SEC is the public's first line of defense against the kind of shenanigans at Enron, WorldCom and Arthur Anderson that wiped out the retirement plans of thousands of investors, not to mention the careers of thousands more. And what did the SEC says in its own defense? That it didn't receive accurate information from the companies it was monitoring. Seems the mission of the SEC is akin to that of a copy machine somewhere in Manhattan. How do you miss a $3.8 billion error at WorldCom unless you just don't care enough to look?

What government and Wall Street have in common is an inordinate interest in the only large remaining deposits of money left in private hands in this country. Your retirement and pension funds. Collectively, government now represents nearly 40% of our economy and is growing at three times the rate of the private sector. Its appetite for money is without limits, and it's trillions of dollars in debt.

This is your wake-up call, Boomers.

The government has allowed once separate financial institutions into each other's business lines and we've ended up with huge conflicted conglomerates that practice managerial capitalism. To put it simply, they can't be trusted. Fact: 100 institutional managers now control 56% of all corporate stock in this country.

Of course, Wall Street doesn't have it its way all the time. My father occasionally asks me to make an investment on his behalf. It's usually in some high-risk derivative. Seems his broker won't sell him this kind of security because he's over 75. In the past, seniors who have lost equity in such investments have successfully sued brokerage houses. Picture a nice little white-haired couple versus giant Morgan Stanley in the courtroom. Guess whom the jury rules in favor of? It's encouraging, but I'm not counting on our legal system to guarantee I'll be able to afford groceries next year.

It's time to take our money off The Street. Put it in local investments, independent banks and businesses. Support good causes. Give it to people you know. It's time to get back to personal relationships as the prime criterion for investing our money, not entrusting it to an institution that knows you only as an account number. It's time to decentralize the greed. Small can be beautiful. Even a small, steady drain of capital away from Wall Street will set off alarms. Imagine if millions of us tell our brokers to cash us out and forward the balance. It's time to wake up to the fact that Wall Street and the federal government are in bed together and it's much safer to keep money under our own mattress.

CHAPTER 7

How Smart is Osama bin Laden?

I've got a brand new set of rules
I've got to learn
I've got to learn
I've got to learn

—Mick Jagger, "A Brand New Set of Rules"

If you want a career in advertising you have to stay up to date. Not just with pop culture and current events but with the big picture, too. I teach advertising at a local college and in one of my lectures I introduce students to the difference between the recent modern era with our current post-modern era.

The characteristics of modernism include centralization, hierarchies, formal business relationships, established teams, mass production & standardization, capital investment in plants and equipment, premium pricing, job security, nationalism and profit-driven strategies. These attributes no longer define success in post-modern, post-dot.com times. Rather, decentralization, informal partnerships, virtual teams, customized and personalized products, flat organizations, minimal infrastructure, internetworking, job flexibility, and value-driven strategies do. Symbolically, this represents a move from away from a male-dominated metaphor toward a female one.

I present my students with familiar examples from popular culture to illustrate the change. The Empire State Building versus the corporate campus, open door policies versus no-door office landscapes, off-the-shelf blue jeans versus cut-to-fit-just-you blue jeans purchased online, brick factories versus intellectual capital, American-built Chevrolets versus parts-from-everywhere Chevrolets. To make my point about the gender metaphor I contrast Murphy Brown, successful because she acted like a man, with Kathy Lee Gifford, successful in celebrating girl stuff; and our move away from a man's man like Clint Eastwood or Sean Connery to current stars like Leonardo DeCaprio and Pierce Brosnan, two men pretty enough to be girls.

Why am I telling you this?

Every year I ask my students to identify a current product that's in the news daily and illustrates perfect post-modern design. Last semester one student got it right: Osama bin Laden's terrorist network. If you think this man is some 14th century throwback, wake up. Our largely modern military is up against a very contemporary enemy. He trains his troops for practically nothing, and then places them in virtual teams where they can evolve and adapt to strike targets of opportunity. He has no infrastructure or visible assets for us to bomb. His flat organization replaces leaders with ease. He is internetworked over the web, through financial institutions and fund-raising organizations, via telecommunications as well as human couriers, within governments and, as we've discovered, through his large and extended family. Al-Queda is low overhead, adaptable, customizable, open-ended and so value-driven (the chance to kill Americans and become a martyr) that customer recruitment costs are nil.

Smart? Osama bin Laden could instruct half the corporate executives in American on how to run a successful enterprise. He is teaching our military strategists.

Not long after Sept. 11, I read a newspaper article that estimated bin Laden spent as little as $230,000 to train, support and launch his 19 airplane hijackers. The same article suggested that well-placed investments on the New York Stock Exchange prior to Sept. 11 would recoup the $230,000 the minute the markets opened back up. Maybe it cost him nothing. He even used *our* assets to wreak havoc. It's hard to count up what it's cost us so far, but a few trillion dollars wouldn't be an extravagant guess and that doesn't count the immense inconvenience and lingering fear. It doesn't count hidden costs like the story I heard from a neighbor who builds houses in Maine. He told me that prices for some building supplies have gone up 40 percent in recent months because so many items are being shipped to Iraq.

When the federal government tells us that this war is going to last a while, that's one thing they're not lying about. Today, 26 months after Sept. 11, our new Department of Homeland Security has announced that it has finally devised a way for its various members to share the same list of identified terrorists instead of the 14 different lists that had been in circulation. How's that for speed and adaptability? Maybe these guys should log-on to a chat room at Al-Queda.com. How much confidence do you have that a centralized, expensive, slow-moving, bloated bureaucracy from the modern era is just what we need? How post-modern do our troops in Iraq, being picked off one by one, look to you?

Might as well be getting our intelligence from Austin Powers.

Worse, which side do you think can keep this up longer? A lot of people are betting on a bearded old man with kidney problems. A man we can't find.

Here's an important lesson from economist Milton Friedman who was interviewed on CNBC not long ago. "There is an interesting distinction between the public and private sectors," he said. "In business, if you fail, things get smaller. You have fewer customers, less money to work with, a shrinking business. Government is just the opposite. When it fails, it gets larger. More money and more people are thrown at the problem. Payrolls go up and so do taxes to pay them. The bureaucracy gets larger, more unwieldy. Unfortunately, history tells us that this almost never solves the problem. As more people are added, responsibilities are blurred, accountability dissolves, layers of non-essential unproductive workers slow down the process and less gets accomplished. All of this leads to a bigger and bigger, less and less efficient government. That is, it leads to what we have now."

If you've forgotten why you hated big government in the Sixties let Milton remind you. The problem today is immeasurably worse than it was 40 years ago. We don't need to change our form of government so much as completely rebuild it. Three quarters of it could disappear and the average American wouldn't notice a thing. We need to put referendums on every state and local ballot to drastically cut its size. We need to do away with our largely redundant county government entirely. We need to get government off our backs and out of our lives. Every time we hear "national this" or "national that" we need to vote against it.

The idea that we can't get along without big government is an illusion. Think your grandparents felt that way? It's time for us to come together again as a generation, not as pawns of the system. We took responsibility for our own lives back in the Sixties. Remember how good that felt?

CHAPTER 8

INSURANCE INFLATION

I dreamed I saw Joe Hill last night,
alive as you and me.
Says I 'But Joe, you're ten years dead'
'I never died,' said he,
'I never died' said he.

—Joan Baez, "Joe Hill"

Americans are so preoccupied with eliminating risk these days, we're easy targets for anyone selling safety. I know people who insure their appliances. I know people who could retire if their dog dies. I know people who make thirty thousand a year and carry two million in life insurance. Why should someone get two million dollars when you die? Will there be that much if you're around?

My grandfather taught me that insurers didn't build the tallest buildings in town by giving you a good deal. Over the years I've carried only enough to pay for calamities. Recently, I've reduced my auto coverage to legal minimums, eliminated my disability policy after reading the fine print to discover that it automatically lapsed at age 60 (just about the time I'd probably need it) and I carry just enough life insurance to put me in the ground.

I'm downgrading along with the industry. If you haven't noticed, collecting on policies gets tougher every year. After Sept. 11 and a few unfortunate weather events, many people have discovered policies they'd held for decades were not renewable, or their premiums had doubled or tripled if they were. What's more, the industry is right up front about saying that if you file more than a couple of claims in one or two years, you'll likely be dropped—even if the cause was an act of nature. Plenty of people have recently received notices that read, "You are no longer compatible with our underwriting standards." And believe me, they don't care how much you've paid in premiums over the years. Worse, your name will subsequently appear in a high-risk databank now being shared by all carriers, so good luck finding new coverage at a reasonable rate. As outraged customers in a recent *Wall Street Journal* story pointed out, "they weren't responsible for the weather."

There's been tons of bad publicity about the health insurance business, too. At Unum/Provident up in Maine, for example. An insider there took this employer to court over a company mandate to simply deny payments regardless of merit. He was fired and is now suing. Mandates like this have become an industry-wide practice and I've experienced it myself. Most insurers subcontract claims work and reward their vendors for keeping costs low—that is, not paying you. My former health insurer routinely turned down virtually every claim I made until I called to complain. I got every single decision reversed. You can bet they've got good actuarial tables telling them what percentage of people won't call.

According to a recent news story, some 43 million Americans now have no health insurance at all (that number is up 6% in the past year). Nevertheless, Americans spend some $1.6 trillion annually on health care, way more than any other country. With the government's dismal history of intervention on this subject, you can bet the situation will deteriorate further. Moreover, the industry has influenced enough Congressmen with campaign contributions to guarantee that whatever rate adjustments they're seeking (Allstate was recently awarded increases averaging 19.8% in 23 states) they'll get.

Trends aren't encouraging. Medicaid is already a major casualty of state funding cutbacks. And if you're disabled or need something special like in-home care, extra prescriptions, or assisted living, all I can say is good luck. Things aren't going to improve with terrorists running around and millions of us Boomers getting on in years. Insurers are going to keep narrowing their list of desirable customers, keep adding exceptions in small print (State Farm has recently eliminated guaranteed replacement costs on homeowners policies), and keep making it tougher and tougher to collect. With better databases (they now use your credit rating as an indicator of your potential to file a future claim) and more demands to turn a profit, they're working hard to limit coverage to precisely those whom they estimate will never file.

Are you already among the millions afraid to make a claim just to keep what coverage you have? Are you paying for something you'll be penalized for using? Is this really insurance?

More of us should start putting aside the money we could save on lower premiums and fewer policies into a personal emergency fund. At least you'll be able to collect from yourself.

CHAPTER 9

THE POWER OF THE LORD

And who wrote the Bible?
Was it Judas or Pilate?
Well one cleans his hands
While the other one hangs
But still I continue to stand.

—Elton John, "Hymn 2000"

I attended a writing conference not long ago during which the main speaker said that of the 45 wars presently being waged on our planet, some 41 are directly caused, motivated or abetted by religious differences. Century after century more people die in the name of God than for any other reason. Comedian George Carlin put it best, "My God's dick is bigger than your God's dick."

How long are we supposed to take to heart the Israeli-Palestinian conflict? Or the mess in Northern Ireland? Or the ongoing atrocities in Kashmir? Or the hatred that persists in Bosnia? Get them off the front page of our daily press and off the top of our evening news. Most religious conflicts are hundreds, even thousands of years old. They aren't news.

I agree with the conference speaker that it's past time to dismiss everyone who sees his or her version of religion as the only truth. We Boomers understood forty years ago that this planet must accept the differences between us in

THE POWER OF THE LORD

order to survive. That differences in color and race and creed and belief systems should be relished. That variety is the joy of life, the very thing that keeps us functioning as a democracy. We were the first generation to popularize the idea of a universal consciousness because we understood that the world is growing smaller at a faster rate than our acceptance of one another.

Maybe archeology can help. There was an enlightening documentary on *The Learning Channel* recently that told the saga of a British archeologist in search of the fabled Garden of Eden. He ended up in northwest Iran at the headwaters of the Tigris and Euphrates Rivers. He found his way there by carefully translating key words in ancient scriptures, both secular and religious. The show was high-lighted by his discovery of an artifact in the Iranian National Museum in Teheran. The object, a carved tube-shaped stone, had been reliably dated to around 5000 B.C. Guess what it depicted? A man sitting across from a woman with a fruit tree between them and a snake over the woman's shoulder. The Garden of Eden story carved in stone some 4000 years before it was written down in the Old Testament. The archeologist went on to reveal that there are at least three versions of the Noah's Ark story appearing in the literature of Babylonia and ancient Mesopotamia, cultures that date from 3000 B.C.

The point? All great religious traditions, at least western versions, find their source in a single story. Only interpre-tation and practices differ. The Jews pray on Saturday, the

Catholics on Sunday, the Muslims three times a day. Moses introduced the notion of a single God to the Jews, Christ to the Romans and Mohammed to the Arabs. Hardly differences worth dying for. To take the Bible, or any scripture literally after it's been translated in spoken and written word over centuries and across dozens of languages is to designate your head as a hat rack.

Virtually every religious tradition, even the Mormons, as related in the recent book, *Under the Banner of Heaven*, has its embarrassments, but let's pick on the Catholics for a minute. Not to deny that the Church has done its share of charitable work over the centuries, but from 700-1500 in particular it was lead by a series of despicable men. They almost single-handedly gave us the Dark Ages while the rest of the civilized world flourished. They presided over a legal system that presumed guilt, not innocence. Adherence was referred to as "trial by ordeal." That is, the accused were tortured. Little tests like putting the hands of suspected heretics over open flames were devised. If innocent, the argument went, God would protect the hand from burning up. After several hundred years of disfiguring people and finding so few innocent, the Papacy abandoned the practice. Rather than dragging the presumed unfaithful into torture chambers, they began sending judges out into the field to make inquiries. These judges became expert at extracting confessions. Collectively they gave us the famed Inquisition. This is the joyless crowd that, for example, identified home remedies like herbal treatments as indicative of witchcraft. They also condemned usury, the practice of lending money for interest — ask them about this today. They perfected the most perverse forms of punishment ever imagined, and hung or exiled practically everyone history has since proven to be a great thinker.

All this time the Catholic Church was professing itself to be the only true religion, the only path to heaven. They still teach this. They have turned secrecy into a fine art. When cornered, they have declared miracles. The wealth and influence they have amassed through ruthlessness is obscene. Some day history will relegate to the trash heap of hubris the Church's contemporary opinion of the rights of women as surely as it now dismisses its past insistence on a heliocentric universe. There, I didn't even mention the sex scandals.

- How about Protestantism? Pretty much Catholic lite.

- Seventh Day Adventists? Still no dancing.

- Jewish or Islamic? Good lifestyle advice if you can get past the prejudice and hate. Seems no one can.

- The Mormons? C'mon, polygamy? Christ in Mexico in the 13th century? Where are the photos?

- Gay Episcopalian bishops? Why not, it's a religion started by an adulterer.

- The Reverend Sun Myung Moon? If you like taking spiritual guidance from a convicted felon.

- Benny Hinn Ministries? If there really is a God, do you think televangelists are the best he could do for earthly representatives?

- Born-again Christians? See below.

Boomers are leaving organized religion in droves. We have sought new paths to spirituality. We have recognized dogma as the instrument of power and control it is. We can tell the difference between the Popemobile and the Batmobile. But not all of us.

Today we face a new danger from organized religion. An assault on what is surely the most important political contribution of American democracy: the separation of church and state. As I've been writing, Alabama Supreme Court Justice Roy Moore has been defending his placement of a monument to the Ten Commandments at the entrance to the Federal Court House in Montgomery, Alabama. How do you get to be a federal judge in this country with such a naive understanding of (or perhaps flagrant disregard for) the separation of church and state? On November 13th this year the Alabama Judiciary Court finally got this self-righteous lamebrain out of his robes. Moore was unrepentant. How do you explain to the hundreds who kept the front-steps vigil in his support that they don't really want crosses on the tops of courthouses or, what follows directly, words from the Torah written on the walls? How do you convince the 77% of Alabamians who polled in support of Moore's monument that they simply are not the chosen keepers of the one true faith? "Judge Moore answers to a higher authority," said one. Good, let them pay his salary.

If organized religion is not going to lead the way, then it needs to get out of the way. Who's needs Jerry Falwell branding Mohamed a "terrorist," or blaming Sept. 11 on "feminists." We don't need Pat Robertson's protégée and the Religious Right in White House hallways, or evangelists from any religious movement. We don't need to give airtime to self-declared purveyors of the "absolute truth" like Janet Parshall who claims she's going to cure, "homosexuals of their sexual addiction because they weren't born that way." And we don't need Army General Boykin saying George Bush is in the White House because, "God put him there." We criticize Muslims for not keeping religion and government separate only to mimic them. President Bush has now established "faith offices" in a half-dozen major federal agencies. The job of these offices is to channel taxpayer money into faith-based initiatives. There is some $65 billion at stake and a hundred social welfare programs that are being taken over by fundamentalists. Senate objection to the program was by-passed by the president's Executive Authority. He simply passed his own law. Feel represented by your government? Even if you're a born-again Christian you should be wary of this co-mingling of state and church. It endangers the integrity of our First Amendment and sets the stage for government control of religion — even yours.

Hasn't the situation in Ireland or the Middle East taught us anything about the danger of mixing religious ideology and politics? Has there ever been a consequence of doing so other than war? Never before in America has it been harder to tell prayer from policy. Like human beings themselves, religion has a dark side and its creeping influence in our government should be a matter of national alarm.

And let's get some new covers on those Bibles.

Maybe a Stephen King thing.

CHAPTER 10

PRESCRIPTION ROCK

One pill makes you larger
And one pill makes you small,
And the ones that mother gives you
Don't do anything at all.
Go ask Alice
When she's ten feet tall.

—Jefferson Airplane, "White Rabbit"

I don't know about you, but I long for the days when drugs were illegal. When you had to meet a guy named Julio in an alley with cash, not check your email for online offers, or call in your refill to Wal-Mart. Drugs were recreational, fun, risky back then. They made us laugh, forget our problems, want sex. We all inhaled and, frankly, I wouldn't want a Boomer president who hadn't.

Recently, I made a list of my close friends and immediate relatives and put a check behind each person that I knew was taking anti-depressants. I had 21 names and 11 checks. I could have had more but I didn't count those taking drugs for on-set diabetes, high cholesterol, arthritis, heartburn, PMS and a host of other maladies. Even still, the number is probably low because not everyone on my list has offered the information and I haven't asked. If you want to measure how important prescription pharmaceuticals have become in our society, considers this: drugs are now the second-most advertised product on network television (yup, automobiles are first). The FTC has passed laws stating that such advertisements must also mention potential side effects and the dangers of drug-drug interaction. Of popular anti-depressants like Prozac®, Zoloft® and Effexor®, these include disruptive sleep, fatigue, nausea, constipation, weight gain and sexual dysfunction. That last one alone would depress me.

I have little reason to believe my list was extraordinary. *The Wall Street Journal* reported that annual prescriptions in the U.S. for anti-depressants have risen from approximately 95 to 175 million in the past three years, and are now second only to antibiotics. Women take two-thirds, but men are the focus of the National Institute of Mental Health, which has, according to a *TIME* magazine article in September of this year, just launched a new ad campaign with the slogan, "Real Men. Real Depression."

Surely, there are many whose brain chemistry is awry and pills help rebalance it. But let's face it; most of us aren't sick, we're unhappy. Just how the hell did we all get so miserable? The polls say we're depressed and distracted, overweight, sleep-disordered, divorced, solitary and disoriented. S-coupes, travel blenders, cinnamon floss, trophy guests and Cindy Crawford's House of Fashion haven't made us happy. Perfect navels, body sculpture and Botox® parties aren't the answer either.

Whatever dependency we may have had on illegal drugs, the one we're developing for prescribed pills is much scarier. Pharmaceutical companies have become some of the shrewdest marketers around and here's what they're doing to make you even more dependent on them.

With a decline in real blockbuster products, the pharmas, as they're called, will be re-introducing existing compounds as second-generation drugs—that is, ones re-approved by the FDA to treat additional, perhaps related, illnesses. Merck's antidepressant Paxil®, as an example, has also been approved to treat social anxiety disorder and generalized anxiety (whatever they are). Lipitor®, says Pfizer, could be effective in preventing heart disease, what about 80% of diabetics die from. Another cholesterol drug, Zocor®, may soon be on the market to fight osteoporosis. Similarly, the epilepsy drug, Topamax®, has indications for everything from bipolar disorder and alcohol dependency to weight loss and migraines. Lipitor is under FDA review to treat Alzheimer's, and the antidepressant Wellbutrin® as an aid to stop smoking.

The list goes on and on and so does your chance of needing a prescription from your doctor, who is being wined and dined right now by the major pharmas. And with the new laws to have Medicare start covering at least some cost of prescriptions, the temptation to pop a pill or two up until the day you die will be more tempting than ever.

The advances in medical chemistry have been spectacular in recent years and I'm not raging against the positive difference pills make in many lives. But should we all be taking something? Especially something that was designed for another purpose and has only a secondary chance of helping you?

What is your natural body chemistry worth? How much does taking one pill compromise your ability to treat something else? How many good chemicals will your body make on its own if you led the kind of life that actually made you happy?

And how much of what you hear in advertisements filled with sexy seniors is actually true? Celebrex® and Vioxx®, for example, have been shown to be no more effective in fighting pain than simple aspirin and generic Advil. Drug companies, like my old friend Julio, are *not* in the medical information business. Even more ominous, the FDA is now being directly funded by the pharma industry, not just by taxes. How long do you think the industry will pay the agency's tab without influencing the agency's decisions?

Maybe it's time to make your own list — write down on one side what truly makes you happy, then check off how often you actually get around to it. It's time to start listening to our inner voices and be ruthlessly honest with ourselves. We're treating symptoms, not causes. We're applying band aids to internal discomforts.

Tonight, take two of nothing and call yourself in the morning. Your body will answer. Remember the yoga and meditation you probably practiced back in the Sixties? Just because you're approaching sixty that doesn't mean health now comes in a plastic bottle. And just because it's handed out by a corporation instead of Julio doesn't make it safe. Oxycontin® from Purdue Pharma isn't called "hillbilly heroin" for nothing.

CHAPTER 11

BOOKKEEPING THE NON-PROFIT WAY

What's the world coming to
What's the world coming to
Everyone's gone to the moon

—Fleetwood Mac, "Everyone's Gone to the Moon"

I 've stopped giving to the Cancer Society and everyone else who's been collecting money for forty years to cure the same disease. When they call I ask them why 550,000 Americans died of cancer last year. I ask them why more of us died of lung cancer last year (161,400) than all the casualties in the Revolutionary War, War of 1812, Mexican War, Spanish American War, Korean War and Vietnam combined (151,200). I ask them what happened to the tens of billions of dollars they've already collected?

According to CBS's *60 Minutes*, a lot of it went to promoting chemotherapy (a profit-making non-cure) and to actively discouraging alternative research.

I have a friend who ended up in the so-called non-profit sector for a time between jobs in the advertising business. He ran a boiler room for an organization that raised money in small southern and mid-western towns. (The fundraising techniques used by most brand name causes aren't that dissimilar if you think about it.) It went down like this:

The local sheriff in each town was approached and offered, for example, ten thousand dollars—five now and five later—to use his name endorsing a local fundraising effort. A portion of the money raised, he was assured, would be used to send a couple of underprivileged local kids to summer camp. Solicitations would take place by phone, no heavy-handed tactics, and the operation was completely legal.

In case you didn't guess, the local sheriff almost always says yes. If he doesn't, the fire chief, or rotary president, or mayor will.

A boiler room is then set up, usually in a motel room or short-term rental. Phone lines are brought in, maybe some portable tables. A small ad in the local paper attracts people who are willing to work in the evenings, on commission and for cash. Folks with no job, those working on other shifts, schoolteachers and housewives typically sign on.

They meet for a week or two in the boiler room, and using ZIP code phone directories dial every number in town. The pitch is straightforward:

> We are asking for $25 to send two poor kids from our town to camp, the effort is supported by our local sheriff, and in appreciation of your generosity we will give you a free box of bio-degradable garbage bags when we pick up your donation.

That combination — local police, a local cause and an environmentally conscious gift — produces a 20-25% hit rate. That is, one in every four or five people will come up with the twenty-five dollars. A couple of guys driving around the zip code with cell phones deliver the garbage bags and pick up the checks as soon as they're notified of a hit.

In an average small town, according to my friend, you can raise as much as $30,000 in two weeks. Your out of pocket includes a couple of grand in commissions for the phone workers, the marginal costs for the ad, rented room and phone lines (the phone bill is miniscule since all calls are local) and at most two thousand for the camp. The garbage bags were often donated. Deduct ten for the sheriff, and figure about $15,000 leftover. Now multiply that across several boiler rooms operating simultaneously and you can see how the folks doing this are driving around in Bentleys.

And it *is* legal.

Here's why. In most states there is no law specifying what percentage of monies collected must go to the designated cause. That's true for the Cancer Society. And it's true for the Red Cross in San Diego, which you may recall, was going to devote a huge percentage of the dollars it collected in the wake of Sept. 11 to improve its own computer operations. The women who was heading up the San Diego office was knocking down a six figure salary and driving a nice car, too, by the way.

Public awareness over this issue has resulted in some charities listing the percentage of funds collected that actually get passed along to the stated cause on the Internet. You'll find they range from 80 percent to a mere 10 percent in some cases. Check yours. And watch out for who is doing the collecting. Fire Fighters Associations and Police Officer Associations often have nothing to do with real policemen and firefighters.

When the Cancer Society calls, tell'em you quit smoking. Keep in mind that marketing know-how has crept into every corner of our society. Heartwarming pictures and nifty names don't make anything legitimate.

Like Chris Rock said, "I've been watching Jerry's telethon for 40 years and the kids are still limping around. Where's all that money going? To keep Jerry's hair black?"

CHAPTER 12

WHAT'S THAT IN YOUR MOUTH? A COP?

I'm talkin' about freedom
Talkin' about freedom
I will fight
For the right
To live in Freedom

—Paul McCartney, "Freedom"

A schoolteacher friend recently told me about the harassment one of her students was receiving from other members in his class. The kid in question was very short for his age. He was also Armenian and barely spoke English. When my friend, the kid's parents and the school administration met to discuss the problem, there was no mention of the kid's height, his national origin, or his poor use of our country's preferred language. Exasperated, my friend said to me, "Do you think this kid would have a problem if he was tall, blonde and raised in Orange County?"

In America, we're no longer talking about whatever it is we're talking about. In Diane Ravitch's book, *The Language Police,* she documents how public school boards, testing agencies and educational publishers have banded together so that children will never be exposed to anything potentially offensive. She says, "What began with admirable intentions has evolved into a surprisingly broad and increasingly bizarre policy of censorship." Censorship against regional bias, evolution, the supernatural...even things like these:

- Artwork depicting mothers teaching their daughters how to quilt was removed because it characterized women as submissive.

- The story of a Black woman who raised money from rich white folks to start a Black school was deemed patronizing and deleted.

- A story about a blind man's hike up Mt. McKinley was removed because it suggested that the handicapped find some tasks more difficult.

Hello!?!?!

Ms. Ravitch asks in her book, "Do we really want to live in a world were anything objectionable to every contending party has been expunged from our reading materials?" Guess that would be OK if we all agree to shut up and stay in our rooms. Worse, just who's doing this expunging in the name of the rest of us? Given what's on TV, we ought to be teaching life drawing in the seventh grade.

What starts in the public schools ends up at Harvard, you might say. In an op-ed piece that appeared in *The Wall Street Journal* last year, columnist Dorothy Rabinowitz lamented, "at Harvard Law today, skill in hard, combative argument is no longer prized, nor even considered quite respectable." Says Rabinowitz, it's been replaced by a new program for freshmen entitled, *Managing Difficult Conversations.*

What ends up at Harvard Law has a way of ending up in our courts. In October 2002, the Chicago City Council voted 49-1 to pave the way for class action suits on behalf of descendants of slaves. Further, to make every company that does business with the city search its own records for any past history of having benefited from slavery, then acknowledge and apologize for it. Can you imagine the litigation that will follow? It's like passing a Chicago Lawyers Employment Act. Maybe the aldermen didn't see the recent poll that stated 54% of Afro-Americans see restitution as ridiculous. A pretty impressive number given that the subject is free money.

Or ask Bill O'Reilly. His Irish ancestors lost everything when Cromwell appropriated land in Ireland some 200 years ago. What should he do, he asked, "Demand an apology from Tony Blair?"

Recently, Andy Rooney of *60 Minutes* caused a political correctness firestorm when he remarked that he wished the sideline female commentators on NFL broadcasts, who obviously knew nothing about football, would consider other jobs. The next day Andy was greeted by headlines calling him insensitive and some less generous things. The president of the National Organization of

Women was so enraged she called CBS and demanded Mr. Rooney be fired.

The problem is epidemic. Within the past two weeks, Rush Limbaugh has apologized for saying the mass media has an interest in the success of black quarterbacks, a remark widely reported as racist. Believe me, if Black quarterbacks increase audience share among Black viewers, I guarantee you the media is interested in their success. Golfer Jan Peterson has apologized for saying that Oriental women on the LPGA are impolite to tour sponsors. If that's part of the game, why shouldn't Jan have a right to her opinion? And be careful if you don't like the war in Iraq—especially if your wife happens to be an undercover CIA operative.

The advertising industry has long wrestled with the issue of political correctness, especially stereotypes. It's a matter of depicting commonalities that appeal to a wide target audience without offending any one of them. Progress has been made. Black men are never portrayed as weak fathers in ads today. The elderly are represented as active and engaged, not sitting in bingo parlors. Hispanic women no longer wear skimpy skirts.

Back in 1969, complaints from Mexican-American groups forced Frito-Lay's animated Frito Bandito character off the air.

I, for one, miss that rascal.

CHAPTER 13

THE NEW AND IMPROVED CINDERELLA COMPLEX

There's a lady who's sure all that glitters is gold
And she's buying a stairway to heaven.
When she gets there she knows, if the stores are all closed
With a word she can get what she came for.
Ooh, ooh, and she's buying a stairway to heaven.

—Led Zeppelin, "Stairway To Heaven"

Among the friends and families who visited my lake house last summer was an eleven-year-old girl who, not long after her arrival, was despondent to learn that there were no major shopping malls in the area. Forget the lake and the woods, she needed—and she was quite clear about this—to be near the brand name stores she loved to frequent.

At eleven, I was building model airplanes, playing neighborhood baseball and collecting stamps. As I've grown older I've developed preferences for particular brands, to be sure, but my relationship to BMW or Ralph Lauren, as examples, is fundamentally different than that of my young houseguest's. While I appreciate the style or performance of certain products, she *defines herself* through brands. They live inside her and comprise her understanding of herself. Trends now travel at such incredible speed through our society that what is hot and what-is-not exist simultaneously—she was in danger of missing both. Being away

from this commercial action was upsetting, barely accept-
able. It was a form of disorientation that no week in the
country was going to address.

Branding and our celebrity culture are closely linked. It
began in the Sixties with labels worn on the outside. It
evolved with the Loud family of California and MTV's *Real
People*. Ordinary folks on Jerry Springer, Ricki Lake and
more recently Dr. Phil, seek and find the public spotlight.
The idea of regular people as celebrities was given a big
boost on Sept. 11 when policemen and firemen became
national heroes. This fall, some 15 of 18 half-hour slots in
prime time from Monday-Wednesday are devoted to so-
called Reality Programming, shows so popular they
promise to change TV permanently. Chat rooms and Blogs
on the Internet provide millions with the chance to share
opinions and stories and build huge audiences. In the best-
selling PC game of all times, *The Sims*, players create a
simulated person or family that helps them through the
day. As *TIME* magazine put it, it's like "taking part in an
open-ended community theater production where the
dialogue is improvised, the theme is modern life, and the
star is you."

Governor Arnold aside, the idea of what celebrity means
has been greatly expanded beyond Hollywood and professional sports. At the Renaissance Hotel in Los Angeles, the
staff now refers to all its guests as celebrities. And the
newest ad campaign for Champion athletic wear features
regular people who only have "a contract with themselves."

Marketers haven't missed a beat in reinforcing the notion that celebrity is within your reach; that life isn't worth living unless it's sponsored. That means time, not just space. Watch a ballgame today and even individual moments are sponsored. Like "High Performance Plays" brought to you by Pontiac, or the "Chance Play of the Game" from Foxwoods Casino. Or consider the hour of programming that preceded this year's baseball All-Star Game. We had Barry Bonds ordained as King Barry Bonds. We got close-ups of players with their families and kids on the field. We got jet fighters flying overhead, and former Mayor Giuliani of New York City taking a bow. Retired players were introduced and given honorary titles like Captain. We got clips of famous people talking about educational moments in All-Star games past. That's right, educational moments. By the time it was over I was nearly sick of freedom.

The lure of becoming a celebrity is overwhelming. If you succeed you can put your name on everything from dish-towels to faux fur. You can arrange coverage for your opinion on virtually any subject regardless of how uninformed you might be.

According to several industry surveys, the average American is now exposed to some 1500 commercial messages every day. One wonders what our capacity for living by association is. My eleven-year old visitor can hardly come to any conclusion other than that she indeed is a brand. First by extension, eventually in her own right. One wonders to what extent all this looking outward will keep her from looking inward. From discovering who she is without all the wrappers, without eventual help from cosmetics, silicone and body sculpture. One wonders to what extent the constant striving for the perfection conveyed by brands and their spokespersons will result not in her fame but in disillusionment.

There is a wonderful speech given by the pastor in the opening funeral sequence of the movie, *The Big Chill*. The pastor asks those gathered, *"Are not the satisfactions of being a good man among our common men great enough to sustain us anymore? Where did Alex's hope go? Maybe that is the resolution we can take from here today. Try to regain that hope."*

Let's hope devotion to the cult of celebrity is something our kids outgrow. That they've learned something besides success equals good looks and money, or that 15 minutes in the limelight makes the rest of life worth living. Meanwhile, let's start talking about it as a cult.

More to the point, as a form of child abuse.

CHAPTER 14

"THE RICHEST NATION IN THE WORLD"

When the money's gone
Will you be my friend
Float a small rowboat till our ship comes in
When the winter nights chill us to the soul
Will you feed the fire
Spin the straw to gold
When the money's gone

—CHER, "When The Money's Gone"

America is broke—we're way over our heads in debt. As Paul Klugman, economist and author of, *The Great Unraveling: Losing Our Way In The New Century*, put it during a PBS interview, "If you do the numbers, we're off the cliff. We look like Argentina." And Pete Peterson, president of the Federal Reserve Bank of New York, echoed, "I see a fiscal and economic crisis in the making."

Simply put, the national debt has risen to such a larger percentage of the gross domestic product that before too long the bond markets are going to revolt. That is, stop lending the government money. How soon? Less than ten years, some say seven. Plan on being around for another seven years? Don't think it can happen here? Wake up, dear Boomer.

It's almost impossible to sort through the contradictory arguments about the wisdom or foolishness regarding deficit spending or tax cuts, supply-side versus demand-side theories, or the true cost of government, but there is general agreement on some data.

First, the federal government openly admits to being approximately $7 trillion in debt right now. That's trillion. And that number, like virtually every government figure, is wrong. The real number is probably closer to $21 trillion. How do I know that? An engineer from Montana told me.

He was standing at the bar in the Black Rose Tavern in downtown Boston back in 1987. He had a cell phone on one hip and a 15-inch Bowie knife on the other. We got to talking. He explained that he was in town to bid on the upcoming Big Dig Project, a huge enterprise to revamp the highway system running through the city. He told me, that like other contractors, he was figuring the real cost of doing his part of the job and then multiplying by three. Back then the official estimate for the cost of the Big Dig was $4.5 billion. Fifteen years later, that estimate is $14.5 billion and the job isn't quite finished. Bingo.

So let's say the real national debt is $21 trillion. Much of the discrepancy is attributable to another economic sleight of hand; something called "deferred revenues." These are obligations to ex-government employees, veterans, and others who have been promised a variety of retirement payouts and miscellaneous benefits for which no funds have been set aside. It also comes from relentlessly underestimating the true cost of new legislation. Medicare is a case in point. The government estimated it would cost $12 billion by 1990. The real number? $107 billion. The government has no budget. They're spending your money, not their own.

Guess what else is unfinanced? According to a recent article in *The New York Times* entitled, "Dizzying dive into red ink," some $25 trillion in liabilities for Social Security and Medicare. One late night back in the Eighties, Congress passed a law that enabled them to divert money collected for this purpose into so-called General Funds where it could be used to pay off, for instance, the interest on the national debt, or to make up for a host of other fiscal miscalculations. Don't try this at home. Collecting money for one thing and using it to pay for something else is fraud, but, like I said, they passed a law. Congress also protects itself from the crap they sell us—with a private retirement plan, for example, that pays them a full salary from the time they retire until the time they die, and then their spouses get the money. And while you and I feed a growing percentage of our paychecks into an imaginary Social Security fund, Congress doesn't pay a dime for their plan. Our tax dollars do. Another rigged game from the gang on the Hill.

Add to this burgeoning red ink, recent projections for the fiscal health of the nation over the next few years. The latest estimate from the Congressional Budget Office is $2.3 trillion in the hole. You can probably triple that number, too, given our open-ended commitment in Iraq, the escalating costs of the war on terrorism, a new prescription drug program for seniors benchmarked at $2 trillion (with the pharmaceutical industry's control over Congress, you can bet this number will rise faster than bust lines in Los Angeles), and a couple of other unforeseen incidentals (did you hear Ambassador Paul Bremer's announcement to Congress that by international law we've also inherited Iraq's approximately $300 billion national debt—owed to France, Germany, Russia and Japan?) Add it all up and, give or take a trillion, we're well over $40 trillion in debt by the end of the decade. Given our Gross Domestic Product, that number is simply unsustainable and that's why the bond market is going to revolt.

So where is that money going to come from? Yup, out of your Boomer pocket. Just about the time most of us are ready to collect Social Security and Medicare, it simply won't be there. And here's the crime of it: I read an article some time ago that plotted how paycheck retirement deductions for the average American would accumulate over an average 40-year employment history if invested at historical rates of return. The resulting nest egg: $1.4 million. Recently I received a notice from Social Security Office saying that my Social Security was now estimated at about twelve hundred dollars a month. I'm no longer counting on even that, and I'm not going to do the math that tells me how long I'd have to live to get to $1.4 million. It all amounts to the biggest rip-off by a government of its people in modern history. And it's going to get worse.

Surveys indicate that most Boomers aren't counting on Social Security to finance their retirements because they have a pension coming. Sure about that? According to a recent *New York Times* article, pension funds in this country are already under-funded by $350 billion. And getting them back in the black requires a sustained healthy U.S. economy. Business leaders are already lobbying Congress to *relax* requirements to keep their funds up to date. Why? Because if they can't meet their future obligations, they'll ask for a government bailout like the Savings & Loans industry got in 1989. That means, whether you have a pension plan or not, you just might end up paying for someone else's.

Not angry yet? Then consider this: What tax bracket do you think you're in? 15%? 20%? 32%? Do the math again. You're paying, on average, about 35% right off the top in federal, state and local payroll taxes. What government never reminds you of is that you're also paying taxes on everything you buy or own, everything you do, everywhere you go, every single thing you use or consume. Add up the taxes on gasoline, on your phone bill, excise taxes, property taxes, sales taxes, meal taxes, recreation fees…the list is endless. And when you die, they want whatever's left. As my accountant once told me, the state of Massachusetts raises taxes every day. According to a recent TV news report, all 50 states will raise fees by $40 billion this year. Heck, in Seattle, home of Starbucks, the government is trying to pass a new tax on caffeinated drinks.

Here are the facts: Your real tax burden is closer to 60% of every dollar you now make. That means you're working until Thursday morning each week to pay for the cost of government. Like I say, it's only going to get worse. Why?

Because to finance the collective Boomer drain on the entitlement system will mean huge tax increases—an estimated 35% of everyone's paycheck to pay for Social Security and Medicare *alone*. It's not going to happen. You're going to get a, "We slid the scale, raised a limit, added an exception, increased a percentage rate" notice in the mail, and a smaller and smaller check.

Everyone in a free economy has an estimated credit rating and the federal government borrowing money in the private sector is no exception. If current policies continue, interest rates will skyrocket, the government will be unable to borrow, and economic chaos will follow. The time has come when we can simply not hand the bill for fiscal irresponsibility to the next generation. The government can print money, of course, (the M2 money supply is already at record levels) but then the average American will pay with a sudden and dramatic fall in his or her standard of living.

And we've just sat there and let them do it. Democracy only works when you fight for it—remember? Battle isn't scary. The consequences of not fighting are. In this case, being nibbled to death. We moved world opinion once. All we need to do now is change our own.

CHAPTER 15

ACT LIKE A PATRIOT

Freedom's just another word for nothing left to lose
Nothing don't mean nothing honey if it ain't free
Now, now.

—Janis Joplin, "Me and Bobby McGee"

How'd you like your children taken from you because the government thinks it knows how to raise them better than you do? I'm not talking about obvious cases of abuse or neglect. Remember the film clip of the woman from Texas spanking her daughter in a parking lot that ran on the evening news in the spring of 2003?

The incident was captured on a parking lot surveillance camera. The next day, the mother's kid was in the custody of the government and she was back on TV in tears apologizing for her actions, pleading for her daughter's return. Not one reporter that I saw bothered to ask if this was the intended purpose of the parking lot cameras. No one interviewed the person who called the government to perhaps ask him or her what business it was of his or hers. No one asked what the kid might have done to deserve a spanking. No one asked what was wrong with spanking your kid in the first place. What they did report was that the mother had been arrested once for shoplifting.

When did we decide the government knows more about raising children than parents? There are an estimated 565,000 children in foster care in this country. Many have been raped and beaten, 89 have died—some at the hands of their foster parents. According to the *NBC Nightly News*, in Los Angeles 740 children can't be found, some are just toddlers. And the Department of Social Services in Florida admits they don't know where *over half the children* in their custody are! Can half of all parents claim that? Just how many lost and runaway children and broken-hearted mothers and fathers are out there?

Here's something else. On CBS's *60 Minutes* this week, Libertarians from a group called the Institute for Social Justice claimed they've documented over ten thousand cases nationwide of our government taking or attempting to take private property and give it to someone else. These aren't cases of eminent domain—the government needing the land to build a highway or dam—these are cases of government officials deciding they'd rather have someone else own your property. Someone like a relative, or maybe a friend in real estate development.

The case of Lakewood, NJ, examined closely on *Prime Time,* involved the town government trying to level a small neighborhood that looked out over a nice park. The city wanted to replace the middle-income houses in question with a large luxury condominium complex in order to raise the town's tax base. To justify its actions, the town had the neighborhood declared, "Blighted." And their definition of blighted? *No attached two-car garages, second bathrooms or large enough lots.* Turns out these restrictions applied to over 80% of the homes in Lakewood.

How'd you like the house you've lived in, for say 20 years or even 20 minutes, leveled so some private citizen with connections can make a lot of money? Listen: When you can't stand on your own property and protect your own family, you're at war.

Get on the right side of the issue to stop it.

Back in the Twenties and Thirties when a lot of the lake camps in Maine were built, a common solution to the bathroom waste problem was to run a pipe straight into the water. That's all changed with regulation and improvements in home septic tanks. Most of the camps have been upgraded since then, but not all. A few years ago, government proposed to rout out any lingering offenders.

Their plan went something like this: a government official would come into your house unannounced and throw a purple tablet down your toilet. He (or she) would then run out to the lake to see if the water changed color. The response from freedom-loving Mainers went something like this: *If you think I'm letting some government jerk into my house any time he wants, you better tell 'em to carry a gun.*

Local inspectors proved hard to hire and the plan was eventually abandoned.

The point is this: when you can no longer stop the government from knocking down your door, you're in big trouble. You're living in communist Russia, Nazi Germany, or some backwater police state.

So I'm in favor of the right to bear arms. There are an estimated 32,000 laws governing guns in this country already on the books and not one of them has kept weapons out of the hands of criminals. That's because lobbyists make sure none of these laws stop manufacturers from selling to distributors who, in turn, sell to known criminals. Any sweeping dictum to keep law-abiding citizens from owning guns is merely going to disarm homeowners and hobbyists while the crooks and the government stay armed to the teeth.

Let's not get confused between owning guns and making love. Let's not put the Bill of Rights up for another vote. *Bowling for Columbine,* a movie that asked why Americans kill each other in such large numbers, was made by Michael Moore, a life-long member of the NRA.

CHAPTER 16

YOU WERE AT WOODSTOCK. WE ALL WERE.

Be courageous and be brave
And in my heart you'll always stay
Forever young

—Rod Stewart, "Forever Young"

Maybe one way to gauge how far we've drifted is to look back. What about those three days of love, peace and music at Woodstock? If we're going to reclaim our country, we're going to need the kind of conviction we displayed in 1969.

Compare that incomparable weekend in upstate New York with the so-called anniversary concert that followed 25 years later in Saugerties:

- We wore flowers in our hair; they wore hockey masks.

- We made love; they made mayhem in a mosh pit.

- We gave birth; they bought *Woodstock Brand* condoms.

- We made our own way in; guards frisked them for tent poles.

- We painted our faces; they spray-painted their bodies.

- We played in the mud; they threw it onstage.

- We had Joe Cocker singing, *with a little help from my friends;* they had Metallica screaming, so fucking what?

- We had Arlo Guthrie; they had Al Roker.

Woodstock was commemorated a third time, in 1999, on an abandoned air force base in Rome, New York. By then, major corporations had befriended the counter-culture because it wasn't counter to anything anymore. Caesar salads were sold for nine dollars, and photos of naked women in body paint for ten. In 1969, we huddled around small fires to keep warm; in 1999, they looted and burned down the vendors' booths.

What we celebrated at Woodstock in 1969 was freedom, so abundant nothing stood in its way. Thirty-five years later, we live in fear of our neighbors and kill each other at an astonishing rate. We've accumulated possessions but lost track of our values. We brag about our expertise but exhibit little common sense. We've replaced understanding with blame. We've built wider roads and taller buildings, but narrowed our perspectives. We make a living, not a life. We've conquered outer space, but not what's inside us.

I spent the summer of '69 in boot camp at Ft. Ord, California learning how to keep my butt from being shot off, so I wasn't at Woodstock. You probably weren't either. But in a larger sense the spirit of the 500,000 kids who closed down the NY Thruway, created a small city on Yasgur's farm, sang, loved and laughed lives deep inside every Boomer. In a special corner. Unassailable. Warm and free.

We're the only generation to share such an uplifting franchise. One that proves a city-full of people can live together with nothing but self-respect and common sense to guide them. We were all hippies that weekend. Living on love, brotherhood and doing the right thing. We didn't need badges and batons and barricades. Woodstock gave us immeasurable strength as a generation. It's still alive today as our inner voice and it's far more important than anything that divides us.

It's a precious gift that sets our generation apart and above.

CHAPTER 17

TAKING RESPONSIBILITY. FINDING DIGNITY.

> You can't twist the truth, it knows no regulation.
> Handful of senators don't pass legislation
> And marches alone can't bring integration
> When human respect is disintegratin'
> This whole crazy world is just too frustratin'
> And you tell me
> Over and over and over again, my friend
> Ah, you don't believe
> We're on the eve of destruction.
>
> —Barry McGuire, "Eve of Destruction"

Whoever thought no-fault auto insurance would lead to a no-fault nation? Today in America you're off the hook. You're not responsible. Really.

My ex-wife is a public school teacher in suburban Boston. Her classrooms are filled with so many disruptive, ill-mannered children, she estimates that she spends as much time on discipline as she does on instruction. When she does get tough with a kid, that child invariably returns with their parents threatening a lawsuit and demanding an apology from the administration. Like so many these days, school administrators work backwards from a fear of being sued, not a sense of right and wrong, so they invariably take the parents' side against the teacher. Good lesson for Little Johnny, huh?

Is there anything from Columbine to lower S.A.T. scores that suggests we're doing things right? My ex informs me that in her school system there are 32 counselors on staff. 32! Counselors for kids who can't read, or hear, or see straight. For kids who have English as a second or third language. For kids with ADD, and ADHV, or some indeterminate form of pharmaceutical overload. Counselors for kids who can't sit up straight, or sit still; for kids who have unwarranted fears, self-esteem problems, sensory integration disorder, dyslexia, cultural, social or athletic deficiencies. Kids with issues. There are even counselors to help kids take tests.

Where were they when I was growing up? I'd have set a lot more records in high school track if someone else had been around to take my tests. Or hold my hand. Or tell me I was faster than I really was. There was *one* counselor in my school. A little old lady with a few dozen catalogues who showed you how to fill out the forms if you wanted to go to college. Discipline was handled by the vice principal whose approach (I speak here from experience) was to take you into the far corner of the boy's locker room and slam you up against the wall a few times. In retrospect a bit unenlightened, but as I recall, alarmingly effective. In junior high I attended the local Catholic school. There, the nuns used map pointers and rulers for a lot more than pointing things out or taking measurements. They took measure of your character.

I watched the evening news with interest recently as our President said the error in his speech about how the Iraqis were building up their nuclear capabilities by buying uranium from Africa was the fault of CIA Director George Tenet and a couple of National Security underlings whose careers apparently had been deemed expendable. The next day the President said he still had the utmost confidence in Mr. Tenet and had no intention of firing him. I can just imagine the director quietly mumbling to himself, *What a guy.*

At this writing it's over two years since the meltdown at Enron. The former president of that company, Kenneth Lay, has yet to be charged with anything. His lawyers vehemently contend that Mr. Lay had no idea about the poor arithmetic inside his company. According to observers, that argument just may hold up and Mr. Lay may never be indicted for anything. Want to guess what Little Johnny learns watching the evening news?

Meanwhile, across the land, lawyers are preparing briefs contending that people who ate a warehouse full of fast food aren't responsible for getting fat, fumbling do-it-yourselfers who relieved themselves of fingers and toes aren't to blame, and the eye- and organ-piercing bows and arrows kids pointed at each other with untoward results are surely the manufacturer's fault. Bartenders are responsible if you drink too much, gun makers are responsible if you decide to go on a shooting spree, and pill makers are responsible if you decide one night, what the heck, think I'll swallow the whole bottle.

We have as our cultural guide in all this the famed tobacco settlement. Under the settlement, tobacco companies have paid billions to states who promise to spend the money to discourage smoking. Actually about 90% of the money has been spent on whatever other projects the states decided needed funding. Bridges, theme parks, whatever. Some was even returned to the tobacco companies so they could—you guessed it—buy better farm equipment to make them more competitive producers. Follow along: Social justice = deepest pockets less 30% for the lawyers.

I can now promise, no, guarantee you, that no matter what your problem, it's someone else's fault. Couldn't pass that test? Not your fault, you were born in Moldavia. Didn't get that promotion? Sue the system for endemic prejudice. Don't like your spouse? Get a no-fault divorce. Got a relative who was a slave in Alabama in 1803? You've got restitution coming.

According to Andy Rooney of CBS's *60 Minutes* there are over 1.5 million civil law suits in California alone every year. People are suing ladder companies when they fall off. Suing diving board companies when they spring into half-empty pools. Suing coffee vendors and pop tart makers because everything is too hot, especially when you spill it into your lap. Out of control gamblers are even suing the casinos they live in.

We are the most litigious society in history and here's what we've taught Little Johnny and his fiend, Little Jane: Cheating is O.K. There's no reason to avoid it, and no reason to apologize if you get caught. Why? Because everyone is doing it.

Like they say in the army, shit rolls downhill.

Last summer I had a new hot water heater installed in my basement up in Maine. I was watching the guy put it in and asked what temperature the unit had been set at.

120 degrees, he replied. *You can change it, but I can't.*

When I asked why not, he told me about a recent civil suit in Maine concerning a homemaker who had left an open can of gasoline next to his new water heater. Unfortunately it exploded and lodged some shrapnel into his son who happened to be standing nearby at the time. The father sued the manufacturer and the installer. The court found that the unit had been properly installed according to code and was in perfect working order. It wasn't even clear that the gas explosion had anything to do with the hot water heater. The father was awarded millions. The court did not point out to the father that gas cans come equipped with tops for a good reason, or find him guilty of anything, say, unrestrained stupidity.

I don't get it. Isn't stupidity nature's way of thinning the population? See all those dead squirrels on the side of the road? They're the careless ones. The ones who misjudged the speed or direction of an oncoming car. The ones who made bad decisions about which way to turn. I'm not suggesting that we selectively cull the population (Mother Nature might be) but I think that when something blows up or comes crashing down, it's usually somebody's fault.

Isn't it? Should we have a legal system dedicated to proving it isn't?

All this costs us money, of course. Take the case of Merv Grazinski of Oklahoma City who purchased a new 32-foot Winnebago®. On his trip home, he set it on cruise control (at 70 mph mind you) and retired to the back to make some coffee. Before long the R.V. left the freeway. A court awarded Mr. Grazinski $1.75 million, and a new motor home. Wouldn't it have made more sense to print his picture in the local paper along with a warning and make sure Mr. Grazinski never again operated anything larger than a snow blower?

Settlements and insurance premiums now put doctors out of business, promote ever more cautious and indifferent personal service, end up in the price of everything we buy. And it doesn't work both ways. When corporations commit acts in disregard of the pubic welfare, they make sure clauses are built into the settlements stipulating no admission of guilt on their part. No blame, no precedent established, no consequences. Corporately and individually, it's just not our fault.

Little Johnny and Little Jane have learned they can leave a trail of broken stuff, unpaid balances and hurt feelings behind them and someone else will clean up the mess, and someone else will pay for it. We're teaching our kids that there are no physical consequences to their actions. We're sending them out into the world with no fear, no limits, no understanding of harm. They've learned that they're in charge and they can't be touched. They're armed with disregard. When they do something stupid, self-examination isn't even a consideration, just speed dial the lawyer on your cell phone.

The social costs are more insidious. They can be measured in taking us further and further away from accepting responsibility as citizens. They can be measured in our disinterest in voting, our increasingly cynical attitude toward each other, our apathy in social matters.

When I was in school they taught us that living in a free society wasn't free. That you had responsibilities. That you had to keep watch, you had to care, or democracy, itself, would fail.

Every day our leaders and institutions teach us the opposite. Every day we get further and further away from ourselves. From the idea that we are in control of our lives. We absolve ourselves of our actions on the road, on the job, as parents and partners and citizens. We have forgotten a very important lesson: that dignity isn't sold in stores. You build it the hard way, by taking responsibility for your actions.

We did that once. In the classroom, in the streets, before the cameras and in the pages of our underground press. We put flowers down the barrels of rifles. We said no, even though we were badly outgunned. We learned lessons that last a lifetime. It's gut check time again.

CHAPTER 18

WORK.
REDISCOVERING
OUR SMILES.

Punch that time card
Check that clock
When Monday comes
You gotta run, run, run
Not walk

—Grateful Dead, "Keep Your Day Job"

Maybe it's because so many of today's jobs are meaningless that we're willing to work three days out of five for the government. Or, as *Boston Sunday Globe* correspondent, Jennifer Berkshire, in her article "Feeling empty after filling eight hours with busywork," observed, "What shocked and amazed me about this job—and every other job I held since then—is how much of an eight-hour day is pure filler."

Freud said that work is the basis of reality. According to surveys, more and more Americans describe their work-life as unsatisfactory. Is it pure coincidence that it's also becoming harder to tell what's real and what isn't in this country?

Blanketing this trend is the shift of the American marketplace away from mass production to a so-called "service economy." Given how well we used to make things, you'd surmise we'd be gangbusters at service, but it's never been worse. The drive for productivity has transformed personal contact into pre-recorded decision trees designed to keep you from talking to another person. When you finally do reach a human being, there's an excellent chance you'll be talking to someone (in India?) who has no authority beyond the fill-in fields on their computer screen. Invariably, this doesn't solve your problem.

Just yesterday it took me what seemed forever to get my temporarily suspended cable TV turned back on. The computer at Comcast wanted to assign me a new account number upon reconnect, and using algorithms the service operator had no control over, also assign me a higher rate for my old service plan. This, despite the fact that rates had not gone up at Comcast during the time in question. Took the boys in IT 90 minutes to work around the problem.

I have a friend whose mother changed nursing homes. He tried to redirect Medicare payments to the new address. Despite the fact that my friend has power of attorney, his case was put on Stop, referred to investigators, reassigned between agencies, etc. etc. Every time he called he got a new pool operator who painstakingly reviewed his file and ended up saying that he or she couldn't do what he wanted because it was "against policy." That's code for I don't have the authority to change the right fields on my computer screen.

The real problem, of course, is that with government and a medley of insurance, credit, investigatory and financial agencies involved in healthcare these days, the opportunities for fraud have increased logarithmically. The last time my friend called, he was told that he was being sent a special signature verification form that needed a variety of bank, legal and notary endorsements proving he was who he said he was. He fully expects to have to supply a blood sample.

Everyone has a story like this. Putting computer systems between people has not only dehumanized us, but it also costs a fortune. Computers can't think, the percentage of inaccurate data mounts daily, and we pay for it in complicated cross-referenced procedures that result in only one thing: lousy service.

The problem is no better at the retail level. Consolidation has resulted in the disappearance of small and mom-and-pop shops where the proprietors took pride in what they did and had likely spent years learning the business. These folks are being replaced with untrained clerks who don't know the inventory, don't know what it's used for, and very likely have little long-term investment in their jobs. How many times have you waited in line while the clerk figured out the right sequence of buttons on their electronic cash register?

Small wonder no one is happy on the job, and the rest of us are unhappy with the job they're doing. With the economic downturn, many once gainfully employed white-collar execs are now doing tasks that make no use of their experience or education. Millions of others are working at jobs in which they have no inherent curiosity or interest. And these are the kind we keep adding to the marketplace.

Boomer women, for another reason, have felt problems with work most acutely: Since 1978, there have been fewer women at home than in the workplace, where the dignity and respect promised by the liberation movement have gone largely unfulfilled. Despite making up nearly half the workforce, women lead only six of the Fortune 500 companies. Motherhood, it turns out for Boomer women, has enormous economic penalties. Some 42% of high-ranking women in corporate America have no children according to the *Harvard Business Review*. Further, statistics from the National Parenting Association indicate that working mothers still retain—by wide margins—responsibilities for childcare and household activities. A lack of equal pay and the demands of a 24/7 business world prompt many to leave before their career aspirations are met.

Shame on us guys.

In her latest book, *The Last American Man*, author Elizabeth Gilbert chronicles real life character Eustace Conway who says, "Do people live in circles today? No. They live in boxes. They wake up every morning in the box of their bedroom because the box next to them started making beeping noises to tell them it was time to get up. They eat breakfast out of a box and they throw that box away into another box. Then they leave the box where they live and get into a box with wheels to drive to work, which is just another big box broken up into a lot of little cubicle boxes."

We saw it coming in the Sixties. Some decided to go grow vegetables in Vermont but most of us got regular jobs. We're now closer to the end of those careers than the beginning and that's good news. A recent *TIME* magazine article entitled "O.K., Now What?" chronicled life-changing decisions being made by a variety of Boomers. The number of us opting out is so large, in fact, there's a whole industry of consultants and publications devoted to the subject.

Maybe it's time to ask yourself whether what you do for a living has any real meaning. How much of it is merely fine-tuning, or dealing with peripheral issues, or missing the point completely? How much of it occurs with little or no reflection on your part? As we Boomers face the third stage of our lives, we're facing both age discrimination and a shrinking job market. We also have more opportunities to do something that's spiritually, not just financially, rewarding.

On Home & Garden Television, they have a show about people who have chosen to live outside the box. They recently featured a man in northern Minnesota living off the power grid. He chopped his own wood, hunted for wildlife, hauled his own water, and occasionally made the trip to town for a few essentials. He was one of the happiest people I've ever seen. No filler in the day for him. Real trees, not decision trees. No weight problems and no wait problems. No pills, no problem sleeping. His day was filled with the tasks of staying alive—surely the sanest kind of work there is.

And a worthy benchmark for the not-so-rugged rest of us.

CHAPTER 19

PROSPERITY FATIGUE.
REGAINING OUR BALANCE.

As we live a life of easy
Every one of us has all we need
Sky of blues and sea of green
In your yellow submarine

—The Beatles, "Yellow Submarine"

Before I owned my own cabin in Maine I made the trip downeast from Massachusetts during normal rush hours. A few years back we had had an unusually wet spring and summer, even for New England. It had rained every weekend and the forecast for July 4th was no better. The day before the holiday, the forecast improved dramatically and millions of claustrophobic Bostonians hit the highways, me among them.

It was a trip like no other—more like driving an obstacle course. The highway was littered with stuff. Not trash, but stuff people had carelessly packed. It was as if every father in every family woke up on July 3rd, saw the sunshine and told his wife and kids to get ready, they were leaving, *Now!* Lawn chairs and cushions, inflatable floats and balls and blow-up toys were strewn up and down the roadway. Plastic gas cans and pails and fish buckets and paddles had flown out of the backs of boats and kayaks. Tarps were tearing off whatever they covered and billowing between lanes. There were parts of bikes, entire bikes, flying off racks. Even electronic toys and computer parts were lying around. There were dozens of other objects so smashed by onrushing tires, their original design and intent was no longer obvious.

We own too much stuff. And we drag too much of it with us. We spend a disproportionate amount of our time packing, unpacking, storing and disposing of it. We spend too much time shopping to buy it and then replace it. We spend too much of our money insuring it. We spend too little time actually using or taking care of it.

How we love *gear.* Advertisers have convinced us that everything from a simple sweater to an automobile is now "gear." We're afraid to walk into the woods without a leather-trimmed thistle-repellent bush coat, hundred-dollar hiking books and a GPS system strapped to our utility belts. We imagine we're Lewis and Clark, but the biggest adventure we're likely to face is how to pay off the credit card debt for all the unnecessary stuff we own.

Personal consumption, as measured by the Department of Commerce and reported in *The Wall Street Journal,* has doubled since 1990. Over-shopping is treated as a disease. At the same time our government tells us it's our patriotic duty.

It's time to ask yourself how much you really need. Fiber-optic Christmas stockings? Life-sized Nutcracker toy soldiers? Electric cheese graters? Pop-up hotdog cookers? Pet strollers? You're supposed to walk the damn dog!

Even better, time to start shopping with a conscience. Think about the 20 cents an hour or 20 cents a day some foreign worker receives so you can own 10 pairs of sneakers, or a dozen pair of jeans. Think about the fact that clothing dyes are highly toxic, and pesticides cause fetal damage, brain damage and cancer. Think about whether what you're buying damages the environment, or enhances it. Think about how big retail, big media, big credit and big oil all conspire to keep you at the cash register and how complicit you are in that cycle. Think about when's the last time you actually *wore out* a piece of clothing.

And think about this: Americans make up 5% of the worlds' population yet we consume 20-30% of virtually every planetary resource, from oil to meat. Still wondering why people hate us?

There's a voluntary simplicity movement in this country for good reason. The very successful *Real Simple* magazine is dedicated, as its publisher says, to women who are "overworked, over-committed and overscheduled." A reported 28% of all Americans have voluntarily "downshifted" already, according to Harvard economist Juliet Schor. You can start by rethinking the list of people you simply must give gifts to each year, and rethinking our obnoxiously over-commercialized holiday seasons. "Christmas," as comedian Lewis Black remarked, "has become a beast that can't be fed. Thanksgiving used to be Thanksgiving. Now it's Christmas, Part One." Start by celebrating Buy Nothing Day, the day after Thanksgiving.

In the ad business, there are numerous surveys that prove owning things doesn't make us happy. After that first blush of newness, most things become burdens one way or another. And the more we have, the heavier the load. Worse, we are systematically being forced to buy more — consider Sony's deal with Blockbuster to have the retailer stock fewer and fewer videotapes in favor of discs to promote the sale of Sony DVD players. You're being manipulated constantly. This kind of commercial coercion is mostly hidden, but it's rampant.

Most people are so buzzed these days they can't do the relaxation pose on a yoga tape. What *does* make us feel good? Control over our life, our friends, family and home, say the same surveys. We have reached the point in this country, the polls indicate, that the "concept of true leisure — contemplative time when we refresh ourselves — no longer exists."

We desperately need to rebalance our lives. To wake up to the fact that owning too much stuff is the cause of our emotional and physical fatigue. It's time to take inventory on the inside. To add up our spiritual strengths as individuals and as a generation. You'll be surprised at how long the list is.

CHAPTER 20

CARS.
A MATTER OF
SELF-RESPECT.

Well I'm not braggin' babe so don't put me down
But I've got the fastest set of wheels in town
When something comes up to me he don't even try
Cause if I had a set of wings man I know she could fly
She's my little deuce coupe
You don't know what I got
(My little deuce coupe)
(You don't know what I got)

—The Beach Boys, "Little Deuce Coupe"

This isn't a chapter just for boys. Boy or girl, if you first got behind the wheel in the Sixties it was pure love. America set the world standard for automobiles back then. Big, powerful, distinctive, flashy and solid. With real chrome and real bumpers. The highway taught us about freedom and responsibility; we learned about each other across those fabulous bench seats.

My father had a cream and bronze '61 Chevy Impala convertible he reluctantly let me drive when the time came and I only had one accident in it. (I blamed it on my girlfriend because of where she had her hands when we hit the telephone pole, but only because my father threatened to kill me.)

I still drive a car from that era, a 1973 BMW Bavaria. Best darn thing I own because I can fix it. The radiator is right there. So is the battery, the pumps, all the reservoirs that need filling, and if you pop off the air filter and get yourself a long handled screwdriver you can sneak up under those beautiful dual carbs and adjust the fuel/air mixtures yourself. Tune it just by listening. Makes you feel great. Something you can share with a neighbor. Compare that to the feeling you get talking to those bet-you-don't-understand-what-I'm-saying jump-suited jerks down at the dealership. What's more the Beemer's seats are high and comfortable so you can see out of it in all directions, and there isn't a rattle in it after 30 years on the road. It's got analog dials you can read at a glance, no computers, no digital controls and genuine roll-them-up-yourself windows. Never fails to start because it isn't engineered to tolerances that would make NASA nervous.

Not only can I repair my Beemer, I can do it for practically nothing. The new headlamp I installed last summer was $3.15 at ADAP. No fancy neon double-reflective gold-lined fog and cruising beam bullshit. Just a headlight. When a friend accidentally broke the high beams switch on my steering column, I opened up the compartment by removing four visible screws and glued the broken piece back into place for nothing — I already had the epoxy.

Let me throw some more light on this subject. You can replace the bulbs behind the dashboard of the Bavaria for about $1 each and you can do it in about 15 minutes. (You replace the light bulbs in your house, don't you?) New BMWs, on the other hand, feature a notoriously unreliable computerized light bar system that costs over $1000 to replace. Imagine, a thousand bucks for dashboard lights. Why? So you can pre-set them to preferred luminosity? Or have them dim automatically when the car is idling?

Like every carmaker, BMW has taken away your ability to care for their product, and in doing so, taken away a bit of your self-respect. Check under the hood of whatever you're driving. Looks like a small spaceship went down in there, right? Do you even recognize the distributor, or starter motor, or fuel pump? Can you find the carburetor? Does it have eleven vacuum hoses hanging off it? Look at the bumpers. Are they chrome-plated steel or molded plastic panels? Are they welded to the body or are they just decorative bulges on either end? Carmakers have saved millions by making modern cars look tough when they're built like Legos®. The American Insurance Rating Institute—the outfit you see on TV crashing cars with dummies in them—actually found Styrofoam® under the bumper panels of one sedan. Care to bet your life at 70 mph on packaging? Worse yet, a lot of new cars, SUVs among them, can't pass a 5 mph crash test without thousands in damages.

Sure, there have been improvements. But not in visibility, comfort, reliability or pride of ownership (the only one I can think of is non-rusting galvanized steel). Worst of all, everything new has been designed by the same CAD/CAM software and the result is an egg. Owning an older car will make you feel like a king, not Humpty Dumpty.

So here it is: Get off the new car escalator. You shouldn't own anything newer than a '89, about when electronics really began taking over the industry. I recommend Beemers and Volvos and Mercedes, the older the better as a rule. The Mercedes C Class is particularly reliable, but you can easily get 200-250k miles out of all three makes with a little love and regular oil changes. There are some good old American models from the Sixties and early Seventies around, too. Cars from California have bodies as solid as the old Ford and Chevy rebuilt engines inside them.

If you insist on something new, try a VW Beetle for the nostalgia. The Mini from BMW is fun, too; I gotta admit it. There are also new gas and electric hybrids, environmentally correct, but you haven't got much chance of recognizing anything under the hood.

Whatever you do, consider dumping your SUV before it dumps you. It's unsafe, politically incorrect, expensive to insure and maintain, and it's depreciating faster than a speedboat. It's the highest profit margin vehicle in the world, so you know you got taken for a ride the minute you left the lot. Besides, you ain't going rockslide climbing in Montana this weekend; you're going to the mall like always. Even the fundamentalist Christians are asking their wacky ad campaign, "What would Jesus drive?" Don't you want God on your side when you have that accident?

Cars are just the prime example of how manufacturers have taken the great joy out of ownership: the ability to understand, care and fix something for yourself. Almost everything we own puts us at the mercy of our service economy and you know what happens there.

These days, I regard almost everything old as preferable to its modern counterpart. Up in Maine, I have an old Dual turntable (with replaceable cartridges and belts), AR acoustical suspension speakers (which have been re-coned) and my record collection from the Sixties (putting out nice rounded human tones created by electro-mechanical vibrations, not "bright" digital electrons). The cabin is filled with old oak, handmade rugs, and pillows, real wood floors and walls, handmade picture frames and old pottery (much of which has been repaired or refinished). There's even an original Radar Range® from Amana that I don't stand too close to when it's humming.

So sell what you're driving and buy a nifty older car. You'll buy yourself some self-respect at no extra charge. You can wax her up, sit back in front of the fireplace, read the well-thumbed owners' manual, and think about how you're going to retake control of your life.

And you can start by becoming less dependent on your car.

CHAPTER 21

WHO'S IN CHARGE?
RE-ESTABLISHING
DISCIPLINE.

Oh, my love it makes me sad.
Why did things turn out so bad?
Was it just a dream, everything we did, everything we had?
Baby, give me one more
Dance while the music still goes on

—ABBA, "Dance (While The Music Still Goes On)"

I don't have any offspring and as Martha would say, that's a good thing. Why? Because I'd like to reform just about every kid under the age of twelve I've ever met. Maybe on their way home from Aromatherapy Camp. While they're still complaining about how they haven't got enough of this or that, or why their life is so miserable. Maybe their parents will watch to see how it's done.

I've witnessed two-year olds screaming to be made part of adult dinner parties and getting their way. I've seen pre-teens destroy week-long family vacations with no fear of being punished. I don't know of a family circle where the kids aren't in charge. We've abdicated so much authority at home that in school kids are instructed to call 911 if they're afraid of their parents. Let me tell you, I was afraid of my old man and dialing 911 was no option. Running was. Phooey on modern psychotherapists who think kids need every decision to be discussed with sensitivity to their needs, explained in detail and justified to death. When I studied psychology they taught us that kids *don't want* responsibility, that they *need to know* there are boundaries and limits and consequences. Kids are smart enough to know they're not supposed to be in charge and that makes them smarter than most of us. If there's a single statistic that suggests this laissez faire approach to child rearing works, I haven't seen it. What I've seen are spoiled brats who appreciate little and listen to no one but their peers and TV.

Maybe if we had some discipline ourselves, our kids would, too. That is to say, what's in your wallet?

Credit card applications in this country number an astonishing 3.5 billion annually. That's 10 for every man, woman, child and dog. Unsurprisingly, credit card debt is at record highs, and late payment fees are a $7.3 billion revenue stream, up from just $1.76 billion in 1996. When you ask a bankruptcy lawyer to describe a typical client, the answer is someone with a 2nd or 3rd mortgage, earning about $50k annually and holding 15 credit cards. Worse, the average American (age 51-61) thinking about retirement has an estimated net worth of $146k and that *includes* home equity. While we're all out chasing a buck we shouldn't have spent, the kids get short-changed. In too many households, parenting today means throwing fast food and a pill down the kids' throats and planting them in front of a video screen — starting when they're toddlers.

I see the results when these kids get to college. Gen-Ys, our Boomer kids, are indulged, indifferent, uninspired by ideas and vaguely unhappy. Many are glassy-eyed from medications. The best of them are as good as the kids of any generation to be sure, but so many more are just hanging on. They share, as a group, an extraordinary need for immediate satisfaction. Where did they get that? From sugared cereal and digital displays? From us saying Yes when we should have said No?

According to *NBC Nightly News*, credit debt among college-aged kids is up 42 percent in the past year. 83 percent hold cards and they're leaving school with an average of $3300 in debt. What are we doing about this as a nation? We're making "financial literacy" courses mandatory in high school. Instead of teaching literature and philosophy, we're teaching kids how to read monthly statements. Talk about a high price to pay for convenience. Talk about wagging the dog.

I see my students suffering from the same thing Black Americans have suffered from for generations—the absence of hope. If we've taken that from them, we've taken everything. As a generation, we Boomers overflow with hope. It's time to share that kind of wealth.

CHAPTER 22

SPIRITUALITY. REBUILDING OUR STRENGTH.

We got loud guitars and big suspicions,
Great big guns and small ambitions,
And we still argue over who is God
And I say, "Hey there Miscreation,
We all need a revelation"

—Sheryl Crow, "Hard to Make a Stand"

Talk to almost anyone and you'll find they're running on empty. For some, it is the loss of our once taken-for-granted security. For others, it is a sense of disorientation. Their personal lives, as well as our collective national life seem out of focus. For most, it is a non-stop lifestyle that rewards activity, but never repose. For us Boomers, there is yet another loss—the growing realization that the possessions we've so earnestly assembled over the years provide no real inner comfort. We have mastered material success at the expense of spiritual reserve. We have filled our houses and our bellies. We're stuffed inside and out, but we hear an echo.

Recently I had the opportunity to work on a book with a talented woman, who despite a promising career in high finance, walked away from Wall Street to begin a new life journey. Rather than study stocks, she studied and befriended the contemporary masters of spirituality—Desmond Tutu, the Dalai Lama, Mother Teresa and Jimmy Carter. She taught and worked with the poor and sick. She became a minister and ran a retreat. She returned to her native Georgia and bought a farm that she filled with horses and cats and dogs, many of them injured or abandoned. She ran for office in her Congressional District, and lost. As her own spiritual strength grew, she came to realize how little our social institutions, even our churches, teach personal spirituality. Her book is about discovering the spiritual moments we all overlook—in everyday activities like eating or doing the dishes, like driving a car or watching the evening news. Her message is that even a few intentional moments during the day can transform your life. Her life is the proof.

There is a vast spiritual movement underway in America that embraces everything from Joseph Campbell's ideas on myth to raising alpacas to achieve inner peace. Meditation and yoga have gone mainstream, so has the wisdom of menopause. At the same time, fad diets, cosmetic overhauls, anti-aging hormones and bionic replacement parts cater commercially to what is essentially the same need.

This isn't just vanity. It's also, as Jack Feuer, editor of *ADWEEK* observes, about our "worldview." Boomers have, he says, "a contempt for authority, an abiding belief in music as a healing force, and an unshakeable faith in the cleansing power of anarchy—political, cultural and personal."

Being a personal anarchist takes strength in times like these. As we enter the third stage of our lives, we need to disengage from our comfort zones. We need to engage in a new struggle, not for more material wealth or emotional intelligence, but a quest for spiritual understanding. We cannot count on our political and cultural institutions to provide a compass. That is noise you hear in the marketplace. Those are professionally crafted promises you hear from our leaders. That is legalese you hear from our educators. We need to work from our own insides out, asking tough questions and following the truth wherever it leads. We have the power and numbers to be the political and cultural revelation needed. We have the personal courage and confidence we gained in our youth on the road.

No generation before us had moved around so much. We shed our parochialism and narrow-mindedness crisscrossing America. We saw the beauty in diversity and understood the importance of social progress. I can remember pushing my old '64 Volkswagen across the Great Plains on my way to Denver or Boulder, the windows down because they whistled when up, hoping it wouldn't rain because the water came in through the floorboards. Outside Moab, Utah one evening, I kept pace with a herd of wild mustangs. It was pure freedom. In the Cimarron Canyon in northern New Mexico I got caught in a mid-summer hailstorm. It was purple mountains majesty. I crashed in rooms filled with people I didn't know. Hitchhiked to Las Vegas. Roamed the streets of San Francisco listening to stories.

SPIRITUALITY. REBUILDING OUR STRENGTH.

Millions of Boomers on the move. Far from home and broke, trusting in the spirit that guided our generation. Applying the glue that keeps us together today.

Many years after that scene had passed I had a conversation in Boston with a visiting Russian dancer. I asked her how she liked America. "I could never live here," she said. "America has no soul."

What we've lost is that obvious. That we have the strength to get it back should be no less obvious.

CHAPTER 23

DEL WEBB, THE DEVIL IN DISGUISE? REDEFINING COMMUNITY.

I love the friends I have gathered together on this thin raft.

—Jim Morrison, The Doors

Wondering where to live out the third stage of your life? On what planet, perhaps?

Pick up a copy of *Golf Links* magazine and study the ads. It's a showcase for retirement communities and developers can't build them fast enough. Practically all claim "to be among the country's top 25." You'd think they'd read each other's ads.

Regardless, homes are typically priced in "the $400k to significantly over a million" range. At the low end you get a backyard that comprises "a beautiful natural tidal basin filled with wildlife." Read: bug-filled marsh that will keep you off your back porch nine months out of the year. For a million and over, you get "unobstructed views of beautifully maintained fairways and greens." That is, an opportunity to stay limber dodging errant golf balls as legions of half-blind, arthritic duffers hack their way across your landscape. I know; my parents live in one of these places.

Golf balls aren't the real problem. You give up more freedom than you think becoming a member of one of these communities. Remember the well-publicized story of the little old widowed lady in Michigan who stopped reading her dead husband's mail and consequently never saw the notices from her development association indicating that he (now she) owed $800 in unpaid dues? Without any further efforts to contact her, no phone call or visit to the house, the association, operating well within the rights detailed in her contract, had the police show up one day with a moving van and an eviction notice. They took her house and belongings because they could. She left with nothing but the clothes on her back and her purse. It took her a full year to get her home back, thousands paid to lawyers, and she never did get an apology from the association, despite the outrages expressed by her now-terrified friends and neighbors. Mind you, over $800 in dues. The bigger the development, the more you can expect to be treated like the phone company treats you. Just the kind of security you were hoping for in old age, huh? Contract details don't appear in the advertisements, by the way.

Fortunately, there are options to this cropping up. Architects have returned to the kind of community planning that actually builds community. In Newport Beach, California, for example, a project called *Sailhouse* exhibits this New Urbanism, which is actually a return to traditional neighborhood design. Pedestrian traffic is encouraged through design, as is communication between neighbors. Porches, town squares and mixed-aged resident profiles are planned. Rosemary Beach in Florida is another example. In

Denver, *Highlands' Garden Village*, with its emphasis on common areas and the use of rental Zipcars®, is another.

Co-housing, the concept of owning your own home but sharing common space and chores, has taken shape in places like *Half Moon Hill* in Acton, MA. At *RiverWoods* in Exeter, NH, residents share meals, health care and art studios. Even Del Webb has gotten the C-word in towns like Anthem, Arizona where his latest development accommodates families of all ages, not a bad idea for Boomers who might be caring for both their kids and their parents.

Community can also be built online. At the non-profit virtual *Beacon Hill Village* in Boston, residents over 60 share a package of services, from social events to transportation, that help remove "the burdensome aspects of life for the elderly that make them move into retirement communities" in the first place.

New Urbanization doesn't build walls. Rather, it purports to encourage diversity in age, race, economics and lifestyle. It's more organic and less planned. Precisely the attributes that have made cities interesting places to live all along. The idea is to "hive" not "cocoon." As my parents will tell you about living in an over-55-only development (where everyone is actually over 65), the only thing they know about their neighbors are their medical histories. Pills and operations are what everyone has in common. Handicaps, golf and otherwise.

Here's an unofficial New Urbanism that my friends and I talk about: the Co-Owned Big White House At The Beach concept. Here everybody gets their own room and bath and shares the houses' common areas. We all chip in for a cook and maybe a maid and maybe some on-site healthcare when the time comes. We've all promised to push each other's rockers into the sun and wipe away any embarrassing drool from each other's faces. No big government, no failing national health care programs, no big insurance policies and no federal agencies to depend on. Some of us have even promised to leave a share of our estates to the co-op so it keeps going after we don't.

Come up with your own version. We Boomers can shape anything in our own image. We redefined community back in the Sixties around individual dignity, global thinking and the natural world. We were the first ones to make President Johnson's Equal Rights Bill real. We didn't just embrace the ideal of brotherhood and sisterhood, we practiced it. We invited non-Americans and Black, and Brown and Yellow Americans into our fraternities and sororities, homes and hearts. We took interracial dating in stride. We dismissed traditional definitions of beauty and status. Hell, we made hair a reliable indicator of social status. We didn't wait for lawyers or politicians or even architects to tell us which way the wind was blowing.

Surveys say Americans are lonely. If so, let's not be satisfied with cool electronic communications and soundproof cars. Let's connect as a generation again. Let's lead the country forward with the power of our single mindset. That led to revolution last time.

CHAPTER 24

THINGS ONLY GRANDFATHERS KNOW

A time to gather stones together.
To everything, turn, turn, turn,
There is a season, turn, turn, turn,
And a time to every purpose under heaven

— The Byrds, "Turn! Turn! Turn!" (Book of Ecclesiastes/Pete Seeger)

My grandfather looked like everybody's grandfather. Thin gray hair, rounded belly, strong hands and gentle eyes you knew had seen a lot. He always wore a long-sleeve shirt, pleated slacks and usually a hat. He wasn't rich or famous, but he was in charge of his own life and at peace with the world and those around him. You could learn a lot just by watching him go through the day. Here are a few things he taught me.

Re-use the things you own. You've heard of rededicating information. Well, grandpa rededicated everything. Broken parts were disassembled for good pieces still useful. Old shirts and underwear became wash and polish cloths. Used nuts and bolts and nails were saved and bottled by category. Chipped dishes became cat dishes. Old pans and kitchen utensils were transferred to garden use. Jars, cans, cardboard and string were collected in a big drawer in the pantry. In fact, in every room there was at least one drawer filled with interesting stuff, including an amazing collection of old ivory dice. Today, I bring my worn clothes from Boston to Maine because of grandpa. A frayed Polo pullover becomes a casual shirt for the country, then a work shirt until it's stained or torn. Finally I cut the buttons off and use it as a rag in my workshop or garage. I get at least 10 years out of a good Polo shirt and it just keeps getting softer and more absorbent with age. And I don't buy buttons. There is something very comforting about helping an object go through the seasons of its life.

Keep your tools sharp. Grandpa's basement workshop was a place of endless fascination. Tools were neatly organized by task, spare parts by household category. Everything was sharp as hell and all metal surfaces slightly oiled. There was no rust in grandpa's shop and very little on grandpa. He could see well into his eighties and his experienced hands worked their way through projects with confidence. I never once saw him nick a knuckle or break a tool or use something for other than what it was intended. He spent his working life as a foreman at Ingersoll Rand Corporation and lived off his pension into his nineties. He had a keen understanding of how things were put together and was fearless in taking them apart. Only once, late in his life, did I see him defer a task. When the plumbing in his turn-of-the-last-century house needed an overhaul, he hired a professional to do the job—in copper, of course. Make sure no one ever has to touch it, he told the plumber. I keep my tools sharp today. I try not to collect them, but assemble new ones only as they are called for by projects. Each one has a history and conveys a memory of doing the job well. Among them are a dozen very special tools I was awarded from grandpa's estate. When I use one I thank him for one of the most important lessons of my life: no matter how smart you are, learn to work with your hands.

Don't gloat over a winning hand. You can tell a lot about a person's character at the card table. Our family game was hearts. All the hearts count one point and the Queen of Spades is 12 more. Low score wins. Grandpa won more than his share of games. He was a man who might have made a good living playing poker. You couldn't tell from his expression what he was holding, or what his next play would be. Mostly, I never saw him get mad when the cards didn't go his way, or brag when he was winning. He taught me the rules of fair play by living them. That you don't deserve either praise or scorn for the luck of the draw. The cards didn't care to whom they belonged, and they changed hands without remorse.

Stay close to the soil. Gardening is all about life and death—after all, which seeds fall on fallow ground and which don't. From grandpa, I learned something else about gardening. We used to kneel together in the dirt in the good-sized vegetable garden he kept out back near the garage right up until he died. He showed me how to properly space each plant, keep the soil loose for drainage, ward off pests, stake the beans and tomatoes, and over the years how to properly place and rotate the various rows. He grew radishes and late in the season we'd pick a few, wash them off with the hose and eat them right there. I grow vegetables at the lake house today, not just because everything you buy in the store is picked so early it has no taste, but to commemorate those early days with grandpa, kneeling in the dirt, giving thanks.

Though I miss him, I'm almost glad my grandfather is gone. He was increasingly unsettled by the America around him. As a kid he had explored the world on a bike and rode around in the back of a pickup. He drank water from a garden house, not a bottle. He had a rifle he knew how to use and his father taught him how to hunt and fish. None of his friends blew their brains out, or planned an assault on their schoolmates. He found friends and solace in nature and in his imagination, not in parentally organized activities. He married my grandmother before he lived with her. He always helped around the house and hung the laundry outdoors. He never bought a dishwasher. His world wasn't filled with unfathomable Nintendo games, X-boxes and personal computers. If he owned it, he could fix it. Most of all, he took responsibility for his decisions. He didn't trust lawyers or agents or even doctors. He knew the difference between right and wrong because he believed in common sense. He lived in a house not a condominium. He was self-sufficient and died peacefully of old age in his own bed, not in a nursing home.

CHAPTER 25

WHERE'S THE RAGE?

Sometimes it hurts,
So badly
I must cry out loud.

—Crosby Nash and Young, "Suite: Judy Blue Eyes"

Got a little free time to give something back? Good causes are about as hard to find as a disappointed Red Sox fan. Here are a few I like:

Environment: Evidence that we are screwing up the natural order of things is so widespread that eco-terrorism is becoming a reasoned point of view. At my lake house in Maine, I keep a log of interesting wildlife spotted on my property. The day I moved in I noted a large deep-woods peregrine woodpecker, and later that summer a deer on the beach. I haven't seen the likes of either since. The red fox are gone, too.

Every year I get a report from the lake association that says the amount of dissolved oxygen in the lake is decreasing. And last year for the first time reports of milfoil, a dreaded underwater kudzu-like plant that eventually kills off everything. Last year the *Maine Sunday Telegram* wrote a long article on the disturbing numbers of deformed frogs being found throughout the state. Frogs, like canaries, are excellent warning signs. And eight whales, a record number,

{136}

have washed up on the beaches of Maine in the first nine months of 2003.

There was also a report in my local paper that an estimated 40 million migrating birds collide with man-made radio and TV towers every year. Prognosis: bad. We're erecting some 5000 new towers every year, mostly so teenagers can carry on inane cell-phone conversations.

As naturalist David Suzuki said on his PBS show, *The Sacred Balance,* "The earth is our mother literally—we are water and air. We are sunlight consumed via plants and animals. The biosphere is fixed. We have become the most numerous mammals on the planet, and we are using up the biosphere at an unsustainable rate. We are not handing down the earth to our children and we haven't been for years."

Again, if you're counting on government to lead us back into the wilderness, better check your GPS. On the evening news last summer there was a heart-warming story about how a fishing boat captain and his crew freed a struggling whale from ropes that had entangled the animal. The government's response? The captain and crew were brought up on charges by the Maine office of the Federal Animal Endangerment Department. Forget that the fisher-men recognized the whale from previous trips to sea. Forget that these men knew about the sea and ropes and were in the right place at the right time. Forget that the whale, perhaps conscious of the effort, actually rolled on its side next to the boat as if to help the men retrieve the ropes from its lateral fin. Forget that they were successful! None of this was good enough for government officials who claimed that only they had the responsibility, the legal authority and the right to assist endangered animals. I wonder how many whales signed a release form giving them that right? And, finally, forget that these righteous government agents were sitting on their office butts at the time, not out at sea where the action took place.

We don't need laws in this country that forbid citizens from doing the right thing, we need laws that encourage the opposite. The fishermen should have been invited to send an official report to the government documenting the rescue and been rewarded handsomely. The reward could come from the money the government spends on buying boats, maintaining offices and paying salaries, dental plans and pensions to people who haven't been to sea in 25 years.

And this was in Maine where most people can still tell the difference between a moose and mountain lion. What's up inside the Washington Beltway? Bill Moyers, on the September 19th, 2003 edition of his PBS show *NOW*, documented the gutting of our federal environmental watchdogs, the EPA, recently headed up by Republican mouthpiece Christine Todd Whitman (she was the dim bulb who declared there was no danger breathing the air at the site of the World Trade Center disaster). EPA's policies are really under the control of the little-known Council of Environmental Quality, a private, un-elected group of lawyers and lobbyists (not a single scientist), most with long careers in the energy and utility businesses, now working for the White House. This helps explain why the United States rejected the Helsinki accords, couldn't care less about global warming, pushed through a new energy bill that lets utilities and refineries off the hook on air pollution, and paves the way to ruin vast pristine areas with more oil exploration. The EPA has been so ineffective under the current administration, that no less than Secretary of State Colin Powell was caught on tape referring to Ms. Whitman as a "wind dummy."

This much is sure. The comfort we get from living with domesticated animals will be poor compensation for the loss of anything wild on this planet. Meanwhile, Maine now ranks second in the nation in incidents of asthma in children. A direct result of the acid rain that pours upon the wilderness from unregulated power plants in the Midwest.

Cruising: While you're thinking about how much garbage you generate and whether or not you should swallow the drinking water that comes out of your tap, let's talk cruising. Here's a romantic industry with a little-publicized history of pollution. Virtually every line is a violator of the environmental rules aimed to control them. It's not just the estimated 400 million pounds of waste that's dumped annually. There's also oil-contaminated bilge water released. Worse yet, ballast water taken on to balance the ships is routinely released later in distant waters containing sea life that's foreign, and often dangerous, to the new ecosystem.

The main problem, of course, is that these ships operate largely in international waters and many agreed-upon regulations are unenforced and ignored. Not much you can do about that. A survey conducted among tour agents after the fining of Carnival lines for environmental disregard in the summer of 2002, however, indicated that the violations would have little or no impact on future bookings. That's something you can do something about. Besides, do you really need a vacation comprised of four out-sized meals a day and visits to honky-tonk ports teeming with hustlers?

Privacy: I have an acquaintance that practices internal medicine in Alabama. He's run the same clinic for over two decades and some of his patients have been become good friends over that time. He recently told me that according to new government regulations designed to protect personal privacy, he now has to assign numbers to anyone in his waiting room so that strangers who may be sitting nearby don't hear their name. He or his nurse now comes into the room, looks at a man or woman who may have been at their daughter's birthday party the night before and says, *Number Three we're ready for you.*

This is what happens when bureaucracies think their way through human problems. You end up with numbers, forms, assignments, codes, categories and labels in the name of privacy. Meanwhile, the government is compiling and sharing every single fact about you they can lay their hands on. Your real privacy is being raped downstairs in the IT room. Your medical history used to be confidential.

Now the condition of your eyes or intestines is available to virtually anyone who professes a need to know. Under the Patriot Acts, your government has decided it needs to know more and more. So while the terrorists are paying with cash and living a low profile, every move you make will become a matter of potential scrutiny by some over-zealous nitwit trying to make a name for him or herself. Wait until you become the victim of some cross-referenced database that suggests everyone who ordered camouflage clothing from this year's LL Bean catalogue and visited a porno site should be put under surveillance.

I tell my students if they're looking for a cause to get excited about, make it privacy. Every time they enter an email address or credit card number on the Internet they're compromising their freedom. The security business is booming, from firewalls to watchdogs. According to the FTC, complaints about identity theft are up a whopping 53 percent in the past year. My students may not care now, but they will at age 30 or 40 when identity theft is a national plague and the cost and inconvenience of avoiding it comes out of their wallet and their day.

And it isn't just a matter of terrorism. Does putting a camera in every locker room help professional athletes concentrate before the game? Does jamming a camera in the face of our national leaders result in anything other than canned answers and disingenuous behavior? Did the paparazzi kill Lady Di? Do you really want fifteen minutes of fame? Better check the price of celebrity.

Voting: I agree with George Carlin that "the shit they move around in Washington every four years doesn't make a damn bit of difference." The sad fact is, the Democrats have proven no more capable of solving the country's problems than the Republicans. As presidential candidate Al Sharpton recently observed, most Democrats have spent the last two years acting like Republicans anyway.

This is why I vote Libertarian. When government gets this bad, all I want is less of it. We have created a huge burdensome federal government that operates with no accountability, grows uncontrollably and already represents a lop-sided percentage of the U.S. economy. It's all overhead and it's breaking the bank.

- We have a Department of Education that spends billions without educating a single kid. Their latest initiative, "Leave No Child Behind", has bankrupted states with unfunded mandates, usurped local control over policy, driven good teachers from the classroom and succeeded in lowering educational standards by insisting that kids be taught to pass tests rather than learn.

- Health & Human Services, for its part, has some 72 uncoordinated programs that have, despite spending trillions of dollars, managed to steadily increase poverty in this country.

- HUD has funded hundreds of real estate schemes that made millionaires of developers while invariably dotting our urban landscapes with slums that breed and perpetuate hopelessness and despair.

- Despite the fact that transportation is almost entirely a private enterprise in this country, we have a huge and costly Department of Transportation. It does run Amtrak—at a $1B annual loss and with a very shaky safety record.

- As for the Department of Energy, see the chapter on Big Oil.

- And, as we painfully discovered on Sept. 11, our FBI, the NSA, the CIA, the FAA and the Bureau of Immigration are a lot more politicized and ineffective than we hoped.

In the senatorial race in Massachusetts in 2000, a woman named Carla Howell ran under the Libertarian banner. Her campaign promise? To eliminate the state sales tax. She was vilified by the media as a nut case. This despite the fact that the Massachusetts state budget, like every other state's, grew uncontrollably throughout the Nineties. A lot of that money was used to hire thousands of additional state workers—mostly fund raisers for winning candidates—to do jobs that didn't need doing in quasi-government agencies that report to no one. Eliminating the sales tax would have reduced the state budget by 30%. That is, it would have been about the same size as it was when Mike Dukakis was governor in the mid-eighties. During his term alone the size of state government doubled. I couldn't vote for Carla fast enough.

According to Tom Patterson, author of *The Vanishing Voter*, Americans are increasingly indifferent about their right to vote. We've gone from 50% average participation to under 37%. It's no wonder. Political advertising has been reduced to accusations and name-calling. Campaigns start too early and last too long. Real issues are seldom addressed. Incumbents get disproportionate funding and media exposure over newcomers. As a result, of the 430 Congressional races, only about two dozen are really competitive.

But we Boomers are 76 million strong! We represent the voting power to change anything we want changed. Wake up and stop voting for the people who created this mess. Get on the web and get better informed. Get over the delusion that a familiar name is better than taking a chance. Chance might be all we have left. As Thomas Jefferson said, a little rebellion now and then is necessary to keep a democracy healthy.

Some other stuff to get excited about: You might consider not buying from the huge corporate chains that are driving small businesses out of business in your hometown. I know plenty of people in Maine who refuse to go into the new Wal-Mart, low prices or not. Get better informed about which companies have a record of operating with questionable regard for the public welfare. Exxon, the sneaker and clothing companies abusing foreign workers, Dow Chemical and Boise Cascade come to mind. And don't forget the Phillip Morris/Kraft conglomerate, which didn't change its name recently to Altria for nothing.

Consider over-population. It lies at the heart of every plague on our planet. People are starving in record numbers, including in this country. One billion people (one in six) on the globe live in slums with no clean water or adequate housing, and at the rate we're going it will be two billion in less than a generation. Despite this fact, many religious groups vehemently oppose any form of birth control, and the right to an abortion in America is under heavy attack by the current administration. Keep your religion to yourself and get on the right side of the population problem.

You can protest the elimination of art courses in our schools and the diminishing tax support for arts in our communities. More than ever we need to reach for art today because it transcends our petty differences. We need to step out of our own lives and reconnect with those that look and sound nothing like we do. Art does this. It can transform your inner self. It can bring entire nations together.

You could get behind the UFO movement. I'm not kidding, and there's one good reason. The United States government is the only major western nation to still officially deny the existence of UFOs. It spends lots of your money to keep every bit of evidence to the contrary locked up tight. Why? Because their vaulted sense of self-importance and unquestioned control will come crashing down with the first documented alien landing. A lot of religious groups will be looking for some new answers to some old questions, too.

Finally, we can get off our nationalistic high horse and begin to appreciate how America is viewed overseas, particularly in Muslim nations. Mostly we are seen via the television programs we produce and export. Is it unconceivable that on this basis we might appear biased, frivolous, shallow, decadent, undisciplined, dangerous, over-privileged and over-sexed?

We can also admit that we have a lengthy history of depicting Arabs as stupid, dictatorial, money-grabbing and still riding camels in our dramas. We can try to understand that our liberal bias toward sex and religion and politics in entertainment is in conflict with most eastern cultures. We're not just a cultural invasion to these people, we're cultural pollution.

We've had it our own way for a long time in this country. It's time to again recognize that this planet and its peoples are in one small boat. It's time for the Me Generation to become the We Generation.

Boomers have walked the walk before.

THERE'S HOPE: CREATING A BOOMER LEGACY.

Hello darkness, my old friend,
I've come to talk with you again,
Because a vision softly creeping,
Left its seeds while I was sleeping,
And the vision that was planted in my brain
Still remains
Within the sound of silence.

—Simon & Garfunkel, "Sound of Silence"

If you've read this far, you may feel there's too much wrong to have a chance at making things right. Time to head for Montana, throw up a couple of solar panels, and get a big toothy dog to guard the perimeter. Don't leave yet. Just because we did our part in the Sixties doesn't mean we're entitled forever. Just because we're more privileged and comfortable these days doesn't mean we've been absolved from social responsibilities now. There's a good chance we're all going to live until 80 or 85, so no checking out at 50. Not to mention the world we're leaving our kids. Individually, and as a generation, we're not off the hook.

Despite our leaders' contrary claims, our ship of state is leaky. We're stuck in a war that's increasingly reminiscent of Vietnam and the body count mounts daily. Accountability has all but disappeared in government and

there's been a complete derailment of corporate gover-
nance. Our institutions have been morally eviscerated and
our treasuries gutted. We're being assaulted by an orchestrated campaign of fear by elected representatives that
have been bought and sold by special interests. Our tax
dollars have been fraudulently misappropriated, and the
national distribution of wealth is dangerously out of
whack. We've abandoned competitive strengths like scientific discovery and educational rigor in favor of political
correctness, which never invented anything. Our mass
media have been co-opted by power and we've introduced
a narrow religious conviction into policy-making. We've
alienated old friends and allies abroad. Our personal freedoms are under siege at home.

Most of all, we seem incapable of understanding our enemies or ourselves, and are engaged in an acrimonious
liberal vs. conservative debate that only proves both sides
are at fault, corrupt and unable to address the country's
problems. As Colin Quinn said recently on his TV show,
"There is no right and left anymore, you nincompoop."

The question is not what *they're* going to do; the question is
what are *you* going to do? Send ten bucks to the Sierra
Club and hope things get better?

You can't sit back and blame the cultural norm when you
are the cultural norm. How many of us were polled last
year as saying Iraq had something to do with Sept. 11?
How many still think President Bush was a combat fighter

pilot? How many Boomers are going to get out of bed tomorrow, believe something else, and act on that?

If social and economic justice in this country has become nostalgic, Boomers need to shoulder their share of the blame. As Stephen King wrote recently in his magazine column, "I think we're seeing an entire generation—my generation, the baby-boom generation—turning off the lights upstairs and putting a sign on the door: Sorry, but I'm taking a nap. Mind closed until further notice."

Five million of us took to the streets in the Sixties to protest an unjust war. We learned important lessons about the power of ideas and the power of numbers back then. Are we now afraid to speak up because it might be considered rude? Do nothing because we've been lied to? No news in that. We never trusted the bastards anyway. There's no sense being wistful about the good old days, they were bad in their own way. What's changed is that government is now so pervasive, our society so interlocked, our lives so inter-dependent that it's possible to control our thinking and our fortunes. What hasn't changed is that we're still The Biggest Generation. With real power, not just flower power.

There are dozens of things you can do, starting now, to live up to our idealism and our sense of historical significance. If we all act, we can remake this society into the one we thought was worth risking our lives for forty years ago.

Here are some ideas:

- Get rid of all but one, maybe two, credit cards. And your kids don't need any.

- Take your money out of Wall Street firms and invest it with people you know and in local projects you can keep an eye on. Build personal relationships with the people to whom you entrust your money.

- Stop shopping at huge discounters; most of what they sell gives off polypropylene fumes anyway. Stop buying national brand names that teach our children that labels, celebrity and self-gratification are the meaning of life. Celebrate regional and state and community differences. Individualism, not groupthink, made this country great.

- Watch Bill Moyers' *NOW* on PBS and visit the show's website for follow-up action. Watch the *Newshour with Jim Lehrer and Chris Mathews*. There's plenty of good journalism and accurate information out there, but you have to seek it out. Cross-reference. Watch for vested interests in your sources, even the ones you trust.

- Get rid of your second or third car and drive less. Be courteous behind the wheel. Your schedule isn't more important than the next person's.

- Live more simply. Empty out the closets, basement, attic and garage. Re-purpose and reuse the things you own. Buy less cheap crap that's destined for landfills.

- Try being more frugal. Try saving string, paper, foils, cloth and wood. Get closer to raw ingredients and working with your hands.

- Live an honest life. Don't cheat because everyone else is—Is that what you want your kids to remember about you? Every lie you tell, every corner you cut makes it easier for you to accept the lies you hear repeated daily in the media.

- Search your community and the web for worthy causes and political action groups. Get involved. Community builds spiritual strength. It's an antidote to the loneliness we feel living with mass media rather than each other. Community creates energy that leads to unexpected, sometimes unimaginable results.

- Know whom you're voting for. Check the voting and attendance records of your representatives. Stop telling yourself there are significant differences between Republican and Democrats. They don't believe it themselves. The "fiscally conscious" Republicans have amassed a huge national debt that Republican Senator John

McCain recently called "evil." The "socially aware" Democrats by and large voted to invade Iraq. Said they were misinformed. What kind of excuse it that? Don't we pay them to be informed? Bunch of sheep is the real answer. The traditional labels are just that, labels. The product is all the same. There are only two rules in Washington these days: repaying the folks that financed your election; and keep the money coming.

- Since Congress will never pass term limits, vote incumbents out. Vote Green, or Libertarian, or Reform, or Natural Law. Or vote for Al Sharpton. He tells the truth plus he's funny. Every candidate is running around this year promising to do something about "special interests." Here's what they're going to do if elected: replace the other guy's special interests with their own special interests. There isn't an obligation-free candidate out there — not even Dean.

- If you want to hear the truth, listen to Blacks. Or comedians. Or even better, Black comedians. Or comedian, Lewis Black.

- Make your own Christmas gifts. Do something for someone less fortunate around the holidays. Think one person, one act at a time. This will eventually transform you and a surprisingly large chunk of your world.

- Improve your health. Stretch. Do yoga. Meditate. Stand on your head for ten minutes each morning. And keep this in mind: it takes six hours of walking to burn up the calories in just one fast food burger-and-fries lunch.

- Stop popping pills. Most of them cause as many problems as they solve. The illegal drugs we took in the Sixties were much less insidious because they didn't carry the cache of social acceptance. And stop giving your kids pills. In an advertising insert in *The New York Times* recently, a large drug company warned that kids who were worried about the future or their grades might be "secretly depressed." Bullshit. Kids *should* be worried about their grades and the future. Listen to the British. Most of the mood-altering drugs we're throwing down our kids' throats are illegal to prescribe for kids in England.

- Stop working for known polluters and companies that don't give a damn about corporate citizenship. And that includes large sections of the government, our #1 polluter.

- Try living without things you can't fix.

- Reduce insurance coverage to legal minimums.

- Strive for balance in your life. Slow down. Seek the spiritual rewards in your everyday activities. Eliminate stress so you can think clearly. So you have time to care.

- Don't shop at, for example, a Christmas Tree Shop. Boycott it. You don't need any more holiday-themed statuary, placemats or toaster cozies.

- Stop living beyond your means and start saving again. We're currently at about 2.5% as a nation, still woefully less than the rest of the civilized world, but better than the 1.6% that characterized the go-go Nineties.

- Forget the so-called New Economy. It was a fraud. Watch out for the boom/bust cycle in real estate. Put a little into gold. Figure a 5% return on your portfolio. Dump your know-nothing broker and get an online account.

- Watch your money. Company-paid pensions and profit sharing plans are disappearing, and judging from the number of lawsuits against companies reneging on their obligations, don't bet everything that one you may have will actually pay off.

- Seek alternative sources of news and opinion. Listen to NPR's overseas broadcasts, for example. Avoid the obviously biased reporting from the left or the right. Listen more critically to everything you see and hear. Start connecting what people say with their motives for saying it.

- Make a list of rules to live by and practice them. Like George Carlin says: *"I have rules that I live by. My first rule is that I don't believe anything the government tells me. Anything."* George hasn't forgotten.

- Tell the truth. Say what you mean and feel. Tell someone who's acting like a jerk that they're acting like a jerk. Get them—and the negativity they represent—out of your life.

- De-institutionalize yourself and your family. Divest yourself of meaningless affiliations and get yourself off databases. Demand privacy policy statements from the people you do business with. Think about buying a shredder.

- If you're at a company that's invading people's privacy and selling personal information, help put a stop to it.

- Volunteer for something. Travel to a protest you agree with. Take your kids with you.

- Start a co-ed Boomer softball league. Or a community newsletter. Or a Boomer "Social Network" on the web. Use the free bulletin board space that's available in your local library or community center to start something. Pick a cause that will garner instant support like action against a company endangering your local environment or water; like protecting the future use of open land or wilderness in your town.

- Give to your local theater group, or support an arts program. Our government at all levels continues to withdraw support for the arts while always finding enough for oil, energy, cars, tires, chemicals and anyone else big enough to have its own lobby. Help rebalance our society.

- Return the junk mail you get to whomever sent it, and put telemarketers on hold, especially politicians. Stop responding to offers for "free gifts." You know what you're going to get for nothing.

- Stop giving out your social security number, including the last four digits.

- Buy American whenever possible. Start a company that makes something that's socially redeeming. There are plenty of great American products. Take inspiration from the stories behind Zippo, or Harley Davidson, or Jack Daniels (which you can also drink).

- Tell your kids to have respect for their teachers and other adults. Whack'em up the side of the head once in a while. Like comedian Don "DC" Curry said, *"No Prozac, no Ritalin to calm you down. My momma had a backhand. Killed most diseases."*

- Show respect for animals and the earth. When they die, we die.

- Vote for every tax cut you can find even if you work for the government. Especially if you work for the government. And no matter who benefits. Tax cuts in Massachusetts are typically opposed by over 40% of the voters. What are these people thinking? Try to name a problem that was solved by making government larger. Go ahead. Try.

- Get ready for some more bad news from the Feds. The government is going to want more and more of what you make and save to compensate for its profligate ways. It's already built sunset provisions into recent tax cuts, meaning they're going to lapse just about the time you need them. Medicare is projected to be flat broke by 2013 and Social Security by 2018—how does that fit in with your schedule? And new taxes on dividends, capital gains, retirement income and estates are almost a given. Add to that surcharges on retirement fund withdrawals and a host of cleverly worded ways to steal your money while calling it something else. And don't think you're immune if you've got a government pension coming. There's already talk in Massachusetts of adjusting teachers' pensions to reflect, not their last five years of salary as has been customary, but their average *career* salary. And if you were planning on receiving a state pension, I wouldn't count on Social Security, too, even if you paid into the system with a second job. The government needs trillions. It's not just going to screw private citizens; it's also going to eat its young.

- Stop hiring lawyers, and solve your own problems. Lawyers only do two things well: saying "no" and selling documents loaded with obfuscated language. Common sense will serve you better. And avoid class action suits while you're at it. You'll get pennies; the lawyers will get millions.

- Get rid of your All Terrain Vehicle, snowmobile, jet-ski and every other gas-powered contraption that destroys the peace and quiet of your neighborhood or the wilderness. Try walking through the woods. Buy a canoe or kayak.

- Fight for the right to remain armed in this country—trust me, you won't like the alternative. And you won't be any safer. Don't believe it? Go ask a criminal where he got his gun and if he, like, sent in registration papers to the state after he bought it.

- Start thinking about a retirement home far from the madding crowd (try not to come to Maine).

- Stop giving money to organized religions, or non-profits that pocket most of the collections. A little research will reveal how many televangelists got their start selling cars. Is your idea of religion a used Ford?

- Watch John Stossell's "Give Me A Break" and Tom Brokaw's "The Fleecing of America." Get mad about something.

- Eat an apple a day. Drink a glass of red wine each day. Stop buying diet books. Dieting is a business with a 95% failure rate. If you stop snacking you won't need a diet.

- Let your kid ride his or her bike instead of driving them everywhere. Get your kids out from in front of monitors and video games. Make them read. Teach them to entertain themselves. Stop signing them up for every darn activity that comes along so you feel better about yourself. Give them a chance to be kids. And stop acting like a madman at their sporting events. Some hockey dad actually killed another kid's father in the stands outside Boston a couple of years ago. I don't even think it was the playoffs.

- Dress up for dinner once in a while. Take more pride in how you look.

- Forget about how old you are.

- Surround yourself with the things you love. Tell people you love them. Call your mother. Create a loving atmosphere in your home.

- Stop going to the mall for entertainment, impulse purchases and junk food.

- Cut down on TV watching. Plenty of research indicates that it makes us cynical, passive, and anxious. And stop relying on sitcoms, dramas and made-for-TV-movies to shape your world-view. Keep learning and share what you learn. Mentor a Gen X-er. They need it and eventually they're going to have a lot to say about our future.

- While 24% of today's retirees still work, a full 66% of us Boomers expect to keep working into our so-called senior years. Pick something new that will make a difference. It's not out of the question you'll have 20 or 30 productive years after quitting your regular job. That's a lot of time to have an impact.

- Stop thinking and acting like a victim. How many times have you actually been the perp?

- Do you really need a cell phone? At least tell your kids you're not paying for theirs.

- Play some Sixties music and listen to the lyrics. Go to a Halloween party as a hippie.

- Stop trusting or mistrusting people because of how they look or where they come from.

- Help get the insurance industry out of the practice of medicine.

- Help get the federal government out of health care, retirement, housing, education, Iraq, your bank accounts, etc. etc.

- Stop being afraid. Stop paying attention to the numbing orchestration of fear-laced vocabulary that spews out of Washington. Wars and warnings and weapons and alerts. As always, our worst enemies are closer to home than we like to admit.

Most of all WAKE THE HELL UP! Stop waiting for someone else to solve this country's problems or make your life better. We're the most self-sufficient, adventuresome generation ever born. We ripped up the cultural roots of this country and we still don't need a lot to hold on to. We've taken more than a few years off, and it's time to get re-involved.

As screwed up as things are, they can get worse if we don't act. Like my father used to say, "Ain't a lot of people trying to get *out* of America." This is still a great country and if you don't think so, visit a few others. Every day, millions get out of bed and do a hard day's work for an honest dollar. Teachers teach. Firemen and the police save lives. Contractors build homes for us to live in. Generous people care for the sick, elderly, and our animal populations. Crusaders demand justice and reporters risk their lives to uncover the truth. In every state in our union, people with very little share what they have with those who have less.

Hell, baseball is even making a comeback.

We deserve government and institutions that respect us, protect our money, and guarantee our freedoms. It's time to remind the con artists, the high-minded, and the fast-talking that we, not they, have the final word. It's time for us to realize we can have any government *we demand*.

Do we still believe in ourselves, or don't we? Do we still *trust* each other? Despite all that's happened in the past 40 years, we should. Youth and age have plenty in common, remember—more free time, segregation from the mainstream, less investment in the status quo, greater identity within the age group, greater political awareness, a tendency to speak your mind and *a willingness to change things.* We were bold, unencumbered and ready to live with consequences once. Now we've got resources, power, experience and accumulated skills, too.

I understand what history teaches about revolution—that only two or three percent of the population participates. That was true of our War of Independence and the French Revolution. And not all of us acted in the Sixties. It's going to take a bunch of us this time around. To get teachers teaching, and bureaucrats out of our classrooms. To get scientists reporting facts, not promoters fudging the data. To get parents parenting, not lawyers and watchdog committees. To put people back into government process, and put lobbyists out.

This country is always better off when we Boomers are involved. We shifted the national consciousness away from an ill-conceived war once before and we can do it again. We need to recapture some of that wondrous Kennedy-years optimism and believe in our nation and in our political processes again. We need to see our future as still ahead of us, and that no obstacle or menace of our own making can't be overcome.

We don't have a choice, really. The alternative is apathy and depression, and we're too proud to exit the national stage with our heads hung down. We've transform America every time we pass through a new phase in our lives. We transformed race relations, sex relations, women's rights, students' rights, workers' rights, civil rights, the rights of the poor, the homeless and the disenfranchised. We raised standards for public discourse and dismissed condescending institutions. We broadened acceptance and tolerance of others, redefining what it means to be alive and together on this planet. We put prejudice and ignorance on the run and lying politicians out of office. We saw things for what they were; we stood apart and shoulder-to-shoulder.

It's time to finish what we started. Not merely criticize pretenders but drive them into oblivion. Not only expose corrupt institutions, but also bankrupt them. Not just trim the size of government, but dismantle huge sections of it. We need to frame America's future in the bold terms of social revolution or societal collapse. Nothing less will work. The changes made every four years are designed to make sure nothing really changes.

As we turn 50 and 55, we're nearer so-called old age than we'd care to admit, but luck has often been on our side. And as luck would have it, the task at hand is perfect for the kind of disruptive, disrespectful, counter-culture, mind-expanding, very cool thinking we're famous for. It's time for every Boomer to dig down deep inside his or her

heart and ask the big question that remains unanswered:
What will history remember of our generation?

Boomers? Yeah, they were the biggest.

Boomers? Oh yeah, they were the best.

Sources and Notes

Introduction – Wake-Up Call for the Biggest Generation

References throughout my Introduction are to *The Greatest Generation*, Tom Brokaw's bestseller, published by Random House, 1998.

Boomers' kids, so-called Gen-Y, are being targeted with music from the Sixties and Seventies in a variety of advertising campaigns, not just those mentioned herein.

The TV special "Elvis Lives" aired on NBC on Thanksgiving night, November 29, 2002.

An Effanbee Howdy Doody doll with original clothing and box was estimated to be worth $1200 on Antiques Roadshow, November 18, 2002.

The first big hit of the Lennon Sisters—Diane, Janet, Peggy and Kathy— was *Tonight You Belong To Me*.

Grunge scene rocker Curt Cobain's Journals was published by Riverhead Books in November 2002. It was compiled from the artist's 20 notebooks filled with lyrics, poems, letters and drawings.

Reported use of drugs among teenagers varies, but few surveys are encouraging. See among other sources: whitehousedrugpolicy.gov.

For special offers and a schedule of appearances, visit Benny Hinn at www.bennyhinn.org.

20,000 paid Washington lobbyists is Martin Gross's estimate in his revealing book, *A Call For Revolution*, published by Ballantine Books in 1993. We can only assume the number is much higher today, a decade later.

For efforts being waged to reverse the effects of "cultural somnambulism," see http://www.creativeresistance.us/media_activism.html. Note: there is corollary malady growing in this country, "voluntary mutism," people who for no apparent reason just stop talking.

When in danger, shop. For one response to the idiocy of the government's advice "to shop or the terrorists win," visit commentator Paul Harris Online at http://www.harrisonline.com/plain/2001/jph1217.htm.

"Waiter There's a Rat in My Soup —and it's Delicious," a history of the Chinese people's affinity for eating rat, appeared in *The Wall Street Journal* on May 31, 1991.

As noted, *Bobo's* In Paradise,* David Brook's excellent and best-selling study of the Boomer psyche, was published by Simon & Schuster in 2001.

Estimates range from 68 million to 78 million, but most agree there were 76 million babies born in the United States between 1946-1964.

As one of many possible examples, see issues we need to wake up about listed at www.voteaction.org/index.htm, the Voice Of The Environment.

Chapter 1 – Are you safer now than you were two years ago?

Both the smuggled uranium and drivers licenses segments aired on ABC's *World News Tonight* on September 12, 2003.

The Gallup Poll that concluded Americans were "willing to concede rights to the government in order to attain greater security" was conducted between January and May 2003 by Michigan State University.

The story about Nathaniel Heatwole, the so-called Box Cutter Kid, was widely covered on national TV news and in depth by *TIME* magazine on November 3, 2003. The report, "Bumps in the Sky," also mentioned the fishermen wandering around JKF International runways and the man who shipped himself airfreight in a box.

Our new Department of Homeland Security claims 175,000 employees, but I figure by the time you read this there will be at least 200,000.

Niall Ferguson is professor of financial history at New York University and a research fellow at Oxford University in England. He is a regular contributor to *The New York Times*.

Charlotte Beers, former chairman of advertising giant JWT, got her start marketing Uncle Ben's rice. She joined the State Department in October 2001, to produce an advertising campaign depicting Muslims thriving in the United States. However, the campaign was discontinued after a focus group in Jordan said the ads left them cold. Others agreed. On March 3, 2003, Beers unexpectedly announced her resignation from the State Department, citing "health reasons."

The leaked Don Rumsfeld memo made national news in October 2003.

A bill to label social protests (such as creating a traffic jam) as acts of terrorism was placed before the Oregon State Legislature on April 12, 2003. Apparently not every lawmaker in Oregon has salmon cakes for brains and it failed to pass.

The *AMC* cable channel ran its special, "Hollywood and the Muslim World," on July 14, 2003.

The referenced edition of HBO's *Politically Incorrect* aired on September 17, 2001. Sears and FedEx were among sponsors that cancelled their advertising. The good news is that Bill Maher will be back on HBO starting in January 2004.

Chapter 2 – The natural order of things today

Network, the movie, was released in 1976 and starred William Holden, Peter Finch and Faye Dunaway. It appears on many "best" lists, and gave us the famous line, "I'm mad as hell and I'm not going to take it anymore." Good advice 28 years later.

Ross Perot ran for president under the Reform Party banner in 1992 and 1996. I miss his charts.

Until the courts decide we can see the transcripts from the Vice President's Energy Task Force meetings, you'll have my version.

SOURCES AND NOTES

Chapter 3 – Why the C-SPAN camera never moves

"10 Questions" for Walter Cronkite appeared in *TIME* magazine on November 3, 2003.

I received the profile of our 535 current Congressional members via the Internet on April 16, 2002. Author unknown.

The Democratic and Republican National Parties are in fact privately owned corporations, registered in Delaware.

Chapter 4 – Musical Chairmen

Much of the information contained in this chapter regarding influence peddling in Washington and how the Pentagon does business, was first reported by Bill Moyers on his PBS show, *NOW*. The episode in question aired August 1, 2003.

Details regarding staffing at the Department of Energy appeared April 21, 2002 in *The New York Times*, "Bush Policies Have Been Good to Energy Industry."

The fact that half of the departing Congressmen and women become lobbyists was noted in Martin Gross's book, *A Call for Revolution*.

Senator Zell Miller from Georgia was interviewed by Jon Stewart on Comedy Central's *The Daily Show* on December 10, 2003. Senator Miller's book, *A National Party No More: The Conscience of a Conservative Democrat*, was published in 2003 by Stroud & Hall.

Over $1B has been contributed to political parties by corporations in the past ten years according to *ABC World News Tonight* on July 7, 2002. The cost of getting elected keeps rising. President Bush has already garnered $130M for his re-election effort in 2004. His goal is $200 million.

Chapter 5 – Was Jack right? Can we handle the truth?

See "The triumph of the absolute fake," *Boston Globe*, November 18, 1990.

Jon Stewart made this remark in an interview with Bill Moyers on July 11, 2003 on PBS.

Several new titles in 2002 mentioned Mike Deaver's effectiveness in managing President Reagan's White House's image. Deaver was a popular interview show guest and made these remarks during a PBS interview that spring. On May 23, 2003 Jim Lehrer, Mark Shields and David Brooks discussed Deaver on the PBS *NewsHour*.

The foray by advertising giant Torre Lazu-McCann into the clinical research business was documented by Bill Moyers in a report entitled "Bad Chemistry" which aired November 22, 2002 on *NOW*.

In 1975 there were about 1500 major media owners in America. Today there are just 600. The vast majority of what is read or viewed by the public at large is under the control of four giant conglomerates. Congress has finally woken up to this issue and is currently fighting to block the FTC's recent valentine to the communications industry inviting even further consolidation.

"So much for the front page," by Frank Rich. *The New York Times*, Sunday November 2, 2003.

The *NBC Nightly News* "Fleecing of America" segment devoted to rip-offs by the telecom industry aired February 27, 2002.

The CBS *60 Minutes* segment on telecom funny business aired December 16, 2001.

Foul Ball, by Jim Bouton, was self-published in June 2003. It is available on amazon.com. Jim told his incredible story to Bill Moyers on *NOW*, November 28, 2003.

A report on web site hoaxes, "Keyword: Sucker," appeared in the *Improper Bostonian*, 2/2-3/5 2002 edition.

The mentioned visit of Louis Farrakhan to Boston took place in October 2002.

The Gallup Poll that concluded Americans were "willing to concede rights to the government in order to attain greater security" was conducted between January and May 2003 by Michigan State University.

"Quality car time with agitator and filmmaker Michael Moore," *Boston Sunday Globe*, October 27, 2002. See also by Michael, *Dude, Where's My Country?* Warner Books, 2003.

Gore Vidal in an interview with Charlie Rose, PBS, November 19, 2003.

Chapter 6 – How The Street beat you

The $1.5B sweetheart deal between the government and major financial houses was reported in the February 13, 2003 edition of the *The Wall Street Journal* in, "Wall Street Settlement Will Be Less Taxing."

The history of *The Wall Street Journal's* "Dart Board" appeared in the paper on April 18, 2002.

Sources: U.S. DataStream Market Index, 1982-97, annualized; and the National Climatic Data Center, as reprinted in *TIME* magazine.

Wall Street, the movie, was released in 1987 and starred Charlie and Martin Sheen and Michael Douglas.

The growing control of institutional investors over the U.S. stock market was reported widely. See: http://www.atnewyork.com/news/article.php/537631.

Chapter 7 – How smart is Osama bin Laden?

Slow progress by our Department of Homeland Security to merge various agency terrorist lists has been in the news since early 2002. In November 2003 they managed the feat according to *NBC Nightly News* and others. Why did it take so long? For rebuttals see the Department of Justice home page, http://www.usdoj.gov/ and its spin-off www.lifeandliberty.gov/, which also provides details of the infamous Patriot Acts.

See: *Terrorism & Tyranny: Trampling Freedom, Justice and Peace to Rid the World of Evil*, by James Bovard, Palgrave Macmillan 2003.

Milton Friedman was interviewed on CNBC on September 23, 2002.

Chapter 8 – Insurance Inflation

Growing homeowner insurance policy problems were detailed in *The Wall Street Journal*, "Hit With Big Losses, Insurers Put Squeeze on Homeowners," May 14, 2002.

The Unum/Provident scandal was widely covered in print and on television, especially in Portland, Maine where the company's Unum Life Insurance business is headquartered.

Statistics on the growing health care crisis in this country are widely available. So are divergent opinions on who's to blame and what can be done about it. See, among others, http://www.pbs.org/healthcarecrisis/history.htm.

Chapter 9 – The power of the Lord

For a rundown on George Carlin's twelve HBO specials, including "You are all diseased," see http://www.hiponline.com/artist/music/c/carlin_george/

Archeologist David Rohl's fascinating documentary "In Search of Eden" aired several times on The Learning Channel beginning in April 2002.

Under the Banner of Heaven, Jon Krakauer, Doubleday, 2003.

"Voice of the Faithful," a Catholic activist group, is currently seeking new members.

See also: www.chessyJesus.com.

This informal history of the Catholic Church was recalled from days reading philosophy at Lehigh University, mostly Nietzsche. See also, *Catholicism and American Freedom*, by John McGreevy, published by W.W. Norton, 2003.

The inherent problem with "one true" religion is recapped in "For God's Sake," *Boston Magazine*, November 2001.

SOURCES AND NOTES

The Judge Moore story was widely covered over several weeks in the summer and fall of 2003. See "Standoff at Roy's Rock," *TIME* magazine, September 1, 2003.

Comments by Jerry Falwell noted on CBSNEWS.com on October 8, 2002.

Comments by General Boykin reported by *Newsweek* on October 27, 2003.

Janet Parshall shares her particular brand of wisdom on conservative talk radio; check your local listings.

The influence of Pat Robertson and the religious right noted by many including *NOW* on PBS on October 10, 2003.

See also: www.AU.org. Americans United for Separation of Church and State.

Chapter 10 – Prescription Rock

The Wall Street Journal, "Antidepressants Remain Popular But Often Disappoint Consumers," June 12, 2002.

"Real Men Get the Blues," *TIME* magazine, September 22, 2003.

"Introducing the All-Purpose Pill," *Brandweek,* July 28, 2003 reports how ad agencies are cross-marketing drugs.

"Bitter Medicine, Peter Jennings Reporting," aired May 29, 2002 on ABC.

Chapter 11 – Bookkeeping the non-profit way

Statistics on death by cancer are available, for example, from the Cancer Cure Foundation, at http://www.cancure.org/statistics.htm.

Statistics on American troop deaths by war can be found at http://hnn.us/articles/1381.html.

The scathing *CBS 60 Minutes* report asking what the American Cancer Society had done with all the money it collected ran several years ago.

The report included interviews with doctors who had not only been discouraged from doing research beyond chemotherapy, but had also been actively discredited by the Cancer Society with their employers. Like Chris Rock says, "Ain't no money in the cure."

The friend who told me about his boiler room scam is Gary Smith. His current whereabouts remain a secret at his request.

The *Chris Rock HBO Special* aired September 15, 2002 on that network.

Chapter 12 – What's that in your mouth? A cop?

The Language Police: How Pressure Groups Restrict What Students Learn, by Diane Ravitch, Alfred A. Knopf, 2003.

"Difficult Conversations," OPINION, *The Wall Street Journal*, November 18, 2002.

The Chicago City Council has had reparations on their agenda since September 5, 2000 when they passed the referenced vote.

Bill O'Reilly on his show, *No-Spin Zone*, September 2003, Fox Television.

60 Minutes, A few minutes with Andy Rooney, on CBS, September 28, 2003.

In February 2002, CNN and *USA Today* commissioned a Gallup poll on reparations for the descendants of slavery.

Rush Limbaugh and Jan Peterson apologized on national TV.

The Frito Bandito, et al, *ADWEEK*, September 1, 2003.

Chapter 13 – The new and improved Cinderella Complex

References to ad slogans are from national TV campaigns that ran during the summer of 2003.

"You, me, celebrity," by Myra Stark, *Brandweek*, May 26, 2003.

References to moments like *"Chance Play of the Game"* sponsored by Foxwoods Casino were a regular part of live Red Sox baseball coverage during the summer and fall of 2003 on the NESN and Fox Sports networks.

Exposure to 1500 ad messages a day (about one every minute you're awake) means everything seen or heard including logos and signage during an average urban day. The estimate is widely used in the advertising business.

The Big Chill, the movie, featured an ensemble cast coping with Boomer issues. It was released in 1983 and produced by Johnny Carson.

Chapter 14 – "The richest nation in the world"

The Great Unraveling: Losing Our Way in the New Century, by Paul Klugman, W.W. Norton 2003.

See "The Tax-Cut Con," *New York Times Magazine*, September 14, 2003.

Peter Peterson was interviewed on *NOW* on September 26, 2003. Among other scary things he said, "It takes $600 billion in foreign capital each year to pay for our deficit. Foreigners, that is, are buying up America." He also noted that the coming economic crisis is also a "moral crisis because of the world we are leaving our children."

"Economic toll from 9/11 may linger for years," *Portland Press Herald*, September 26, 2003.

As of November 14, 2003, the tabulated national debt is $6,870,815,186,447. Your personal share is over $70,000 and growing.

Cost of Medicare figure taken from "Can we afford all this?" *TIME* magazine, December 8, 2003.

"Dizzying Dive Into Red Ink Poses Stark Choices for Washington," *The New York Times*, September 14, 2003.

How Congress looks after itself at our expense when it comes to retirement has been widely reported. References were taken from "FICA and Social Security" distributed via the Internet on May 13, 2003, author unknown.

Congressional Budget Office estimates were taken from "Deficits: Danger Ahead?" which appeared in the *AARP Bulletin*, May 2003.

The article I read some years back estimated that the average American worker would have $1.4 million dollars at retirement if it *weren't* for Social Security.

The New York Times, December 7, 2003, "Pension Troubles=S.&L. Collapse? Some say bank on it."

My estimate says you're now paying close to 60% of your income in taxes of all kinds. You do the math.

References to your future tax burden were culled from: "The Really Unfair Tax," *TIME* magazine, February 3, 2003; "Deficits and Dysfunction: How the Republicans (and Democrats) Have Sold Out Our Future," *New York Times Magazine*, June 8, 2003; *Fidelity Investments Newsletter*, June 8, 2001; and "The Losing 'War' on the Estate Tax," by Thomas Oliphant, *Boston Sunday Globe*, June 16, 2002.

Chapter 15 – Act like a Patriot

The references to *NBC Nightly News*, *60 Minutes* on CBS and ABC's *Prime Time* were all broadcasts that aired during October 2003.

Gun Laws in America, Alan Korwin, Bloomfield Press 2000. The number of gun laws in America grows approximately 6% a year.

Visit the National Rifle Association at: www.nra.org. Be patient, it loads slowly.

Bowling for Columbine, the movie, was released in 2003 and won the Academy Award for Best Documentary.

Chapter 16 – You were at Woodstock. We all were.

Videos from Woodstock 1994 and Woodstock 1999 are readily available online. If you're like me, you've still got the original video and LP.

"Woodstock Envy," *AARP Magazine*, March & April 2002.

Chapter 17 – Taking Responsibility. Finding Dignity.

I attended St. Katherine of Sienna Parochial School in Wayne, PA for two years. The nun who beat me with a map pointer was Sister Mary Benigna. I can still see her face.

The flap between the CIA and the White House over African uranium (or not) was widely reported in the national media.

References to absurd lawsuits were culled from: "Gambling on the Court," *The Wall Street Journal*, October 22, 2002; "If Students Cheat, Change the Test," letters to *The New York Times*, September 4, 2003; "Fat Foods: Back in Court," *TIME* magazine, September 2003; and the annual "Stella Awards" distributed over the Internet, January 27, 2003.

References to the Big Tobacco settlement appeared in Dave Barry's column, "Cough it up," *Boston Globe Magazine*, September 22, 2002.

Andy Rooney's comments on civil suits aired on *60 Minutes* in October 2003.

Chapter 18 – Work. Rediscovering our smiles.

"Feeling empty after filling eight hours with lousy work," *Boston Sunday Globe*, June 9, 2002.

"We work too hard," *Boston Magazine*, November 2001.

Women's employment issues appeared in the following publications: "Women Boomers acknowledge gains, slights," *Boston Sunday Globe*, October 6, 2002; and "Executive Women and the <u>Myth</u> of Having It All," *Harvard Business Review*, April 2002.

See also, *Great Expectations: America and the Baby Boom Generation* by Landon Jones, Ballantine Books, 1981.

The Last American Man, by Elizabeth Gilbert, Viking Press, 2002.

"O.K., Now What?" appeared in the June 2003 "Generations" bonus section of *TIME* magazine.

"Layoffs and Lattes," *The Wall Street Journal,* March 14, 2003.

The story about call centers and off-shoring American service jobs aired on *NOW,* August 29, 2003, on PBS stations.

Chapter 19 – Prosperity fatigue. Regaining our balance.

The phrase "prosperity fatigue" first came to my attention in Debra Goldman's "Consumer Republic" column, *ADWEEK,* February 4, 2002.

Personal consumption is measured by the Department of Commerce and statistics are available at http://www.infoplease.com/ipa/A0104550.html.

Voluntary Simplicity, by Duane Elgin, William Morrow 1993.

"Learning To Make Do With Less," *The Chronicle of Philanthropy,* September 7, 2000.

"Downsizing Christmas — Nice Idea, Difficult To Execute," *The Wall Street Journal,* December 2, 2002.

"Too Much Stuff," *Boston Sunday Globe,* December 8, 2002.

"They Care About the World (and They Shop, Too)," *New York Sunday Times,* July 20, 2003.

The SONY/Blockbuster deal was told to me by a Blockbuster clerk in Windham, ME.

Surveys about what really makes us happy are common in the advertising business. See confirming data in *TIME* magazine's, "No Price on Happiness," September 8, 2003.

The mentioned poll and the issue of time and happiness were discussed in detail in The *Wall Street Journal's* special section "American Opinion," published March 8, 1996.

Chapter 20 – Cars. A matter of self-respect.

"If Not A Love Affair With Our Cars, A Very Time-Consuming Marriage," *ADWEEK*, September 15, 2003.

"Can Detroit Make Cars That Baby Boomers Like?" *Business Week*, December 1, 1997.

The dangers of SUVs have been widely reported, including "Auto Safety Czar Warns Drivers of SUV Dangers," *The Wall Street Journal*, January 15, 2002.

Chapter 21 – Who's in charge? Re-establishing discipline.

Kids' attitudes were examined by Peter Jennings on an *ABC News Special*, "In Search of America" which aired September 5, 2002.

Credit card debt held by Americans is documented regularly in the press. See http://news.google.com/news?q=credit+card+debt+bankruptcy&hl=en&lr=&i e=UTF-8&sa=N&tab=nn.

For many quoted facts in this chapter see, "Medicating Young Minds," *TIME* magazine, November 3, 2003; and "Struggle of the Classes," *TIME* magazine, September 22, 2003.

The *NBC Nightly News* report on college kids and credit card debt aired on December 11, 2003.

Chapter 22 – Spirituality. Rebuilding our strength.

"The Party Line on Flab," *Harvard Magazine*, September-October 2002.

"I can't sleep," *The Wall Street Journal*, June 7, 2002.

Alter Your Life: How to turn everyday activities into spirituality rewarding experiences, by Dr. Kathleen Hall, www.alteryourlife.com.

"Boomers' Rebel Yell," *ADWEEK*, July 28, 2003.

"Just Say Om," *TIME* magazine, August 4, 2003.

See also, *Why your Life Sucks*, by Alan Cohen, Jodere Books 2003.

Chapter 23 – Del Webb, the devil in disguise? Redefining community.

Sailhouse: "Developer bets on distinctive design in Corona del Mar," *The New York Times*, February 24, 2002.

Highlands Garden Village: "Smart Denver Project Gets High Marks," *The Wall Street Journal*, March 12, 2003.

Half Moon Hill: "Co-housing Concept Grows in Mass.," *Boston Sunday Globe*, March 12, 2003.

RiverWoods: "A Pair's Persistence Pays Off," *The New York Times*, March 18, 2003.

Beacon Hill Village: "Beacon Hill Village offers virtual retirement community," *The Beacon Hill Times*, December 4, 2001.

Chapter 24 – Things only grandfathers know

"Obituary for Common Sense," distributed via the Internet in August 2002, author unknown.

Chapter 25 – Where's the rage?

"Frog deformities, die-offs alarm scientist at parks," *Maine Sunday Telegram*, June 16, 2002.

"Ornithologist's Nightmare," aired on *New Hampshire Public Television*, January 14, 2003.

The story about the Federal Animal Endangerment Department and the whale was reported on local news stations in Portland, ME during the summer of 2003.

White House control over the EPA was reported on *NOW* September 19, 2003, PBS stations.

"For Cruise Ships, A History of Pollution," *The New York Times*, June 16, 2002.

"Privacy, The Internet Wants Your Personal Info," *Business Week*, April 5, 1999.

See also: www.freedomofinfo.org.

"Freedom. Just another word for nothing left to lose," revealed the government's efforts to create a national ID system, in the *Portland Phoenix*, July 12, 2002.

The profiles of various federal departments were presented in Martin Gross's book, *A Call for Revolution*, Ballantine Books 1993.

"Fighting City Hall," discussed big chains versus local retailers in the May 2002 edition of *Forbes Small Business (FSB)*.

At the time of this writing President Bush is waging a legal battle with several courts to restrict a woman's right to have a late-term abortion.

According to a Roper poll, one in every seven Americans claims to have had, or knows someone who has had, an encounter with an UFO.

"Hollywood and the Muslim World," an *AMC* Project aired on July 14, 2003.

See also, "The Peace Brokers: Ad Execs Can Still Help American Diplomacy in the Arab World," *ADWEEK*, June 23, 2003.

Conclusion – Creating a Boomer Legacy

Stephen King writes for Entertainment Weekly. *PWDaily online* referenced his remark on December 2, 2003.

Living within your means? Annual late-fee revenues on credit cards jumped from $1.7B in 1996 to a record $7.3B last year as noted in *The Wall Street Journal*, May 21, 2002.

Money and the Meaning of Life, Jacob Needleman, Currency press 1994.

There are some decent politicians out there. Republican Governor Bob Riley in Alabama, for example, wants to reduce taxes on the poor and greatly increase them for the wealthy. Charles Shuman (D-NY) is fighting the atrocious energy bill now before Congress that provides legal immunity to the manufacturers of the MTBE additive in gasoline that has polluted lake and drinking water in 36 states. The bill even provides a $2B grant to this industry for going out of business. Ever wonder why small businesses don't get paid for going out of business?

Lewis Black is a funny man who tells the truth. He has several CDs on the market.

Health care is now the main economic engine in this economy, yet everyone agrees it's in crisis mode. Better start looking after yourself; you can't afford their solution. See "Health Care As Main Engine: Is That So Bad?" *The New York Times*, November 11, 2001.

For some reliable health information, see the Center for Science in the Public Interest, www.cspinet.org.

A consortium of pharmas sponsored the advertising insert referred to. Entitled "from cause to cure," it ran in *The New York Times* in fall of 2003.

On *48 Hours*, September 2, 2002, CBS covered the massive over-prescription of antibiotics that's resulted in resistance by common bacteria that give us things like pneumonia and ear infections.

Besides *Real Simple*, see *Everyday Food*, *Budget Living*, *Organic Style*, *Enlightenment Magazine*, *Body & Soul*, *og*, and *yoga Journal*.

For a comparison of on-line brokerage services, see, "How the Sites Stack Up," *Business Week*, September 22, 1997.

SOURCES AND NOTES

"Retirees ask for justice from Polaroid," *Boston Sunday Globe*, December 9, 2001.

The *Utne Reader* is online at www.utne.com.

Your right to privacy is under attack from every quarter. A Google search reveals current information. Note: Delaware has become the first state to begin keeping lists of people who *might* commit a crime. Sounds like a Tom Cruise movie to me.

Returning junk mail and sending in incomplete responses costs direct mailers postage both ways.

Keep this in mind: A lot of people asking for your social security number don't have the right to demand it. That includes the Department of Motor Vehicles. Ask that an alternate number be assigned.

Visit: the Leave Us Alone Coalition at, http://www.libertyhaven.com/

In the Massachusetts November 2002 elections, 53% voted to *keep* the state sales tax!

The crisis in Social Security and Medicare funding is being hotly debated. Given the government's track record, do you really want them handling prescription drug benefits or, worse, some form of nationalized health care?

For information on income distribution, visit, http://www.ufenet.org/

For arguments regarding gun control, see www.nra.org.

The diet industry in this country is an over $40B marketplace with a 95% failure rate.

Complaints about age bias in employment are skyrocketing. See www.eeoc.gov, www.aarp.com, www.nolo.com, www.40plus-dc.com.

There are plenty of Boomer sites on the Internet: www.ThirdAge.com, for example.

For the joys of becoming a grandparent, see "It's About Pure Love," by Gail Sheehy in *Parade Magazine,* May 12, 2002.

"Don't Trust Anyone Under 30: Boomers Struggle With Their New Role as Mentors," *The Wall Street Journal,* June 5, 2002.

Due to budget cuts, some 900 Boston Public School teachers were fired in 2003.

For lots of ideas and resources on how to become a more involved citizen, go to www.pbs.org/now/resolutions.html.

For another take on the day's headlines, see www.Alternet.org.

ACKNOWLEDGMENTS

Like every writer, I'm sustained and encouraged by actual and extended families. They include, first off, my parents, who set high standards for themselves and insisted I do the same. They gave me an appreciation for this country and taught me the importance of giving back.

Also included are many friends, particularly my "Big Chill" group from Iowa City—Wally, Doc, Richard, Satch, Marshall, Melanie and Barry.

Thanks also to those who helped assemble the book, including Tom and Janet Neville for their fine design, Cynthia Cohen for her insightful feedback, Jules Fried who gave me both good advice and the means to pursue the work, to Nancy Farrington and Joanne Murrman for their informal clipping services, and Gerri D'Ovidio for her careful proofreading.

Thanks also to my writing group in Maine: Mari, Lindsay, Harriet and Mike who read early chapters and helped get this project off to a good start. To Tori and Louise, friends from the Bennington writers workshop for their encouragement and confidence.

Finally, to all the Boomers out there who believe that our generation has a special place in history.

ORDER FORM
(photo copy this page)

BY CREDIT CARD ONLINE: *Amazon.com*

	Qty.	Total
I WAS MUCH HAPPIER WHEN EVERYTHING I OWNED WAS IN THE BACK SEAT OF MY VOLKSWAGEN: A WAKE-UP CALL FOR THE BIGGEST GENERATION		
$14.95 (USA) $18.95 (CAN)	_____	_____
Sales Tax (MA residents) $ .70 per book		_____
Shipping (up to 2 books)		$ _3.75_
TOTAL		$ _____

BY CHECK: **Note! Make checks payable to Informed Sources, Inc.**

Ship to:

Name _____

Mailing Address _____

_____

City_____State _____ Zip _____

Daytime Phone _____

Email address_____

Mail to: Baby Boomer Press, P.O. Box 290145, Charlestown, MA 02129

BY PHONE: For more information, or quantity and promotional discounts, call: **1-800-507-1968.**

Please note: We have no refund or exchange policy.